Sean O'Faolain's Irish Vision

Sean O'Faolain's Irish Vision

RICHARD BONACCORSO

State University of New York Press

In Memory
James A. Bonaccorso

Published by
State University of New York Press, Albany

© 1987 State University of New York

For information, address State University of New York
Press, State University Plaza, Albany, N.Y., 12246

Library of Congress Cataloging in Publication Data

Bonaccorso, Richard, 1941-
     Sean O'Faolain's Irish vision.

     Bibliography: p.
     Includes index.
     1. O'Faoláin, Seán, 1900-   —Criticism and
interpretation.   2. Ireland in literature.   I. Title.
PR6029.F3Z59   1987   823'.912   87-10014
ISBN 0-88706-536-8
ISBN 0-88706-537-6 (pbk.)

10 9 8 7 6 5 4 3 2 1

Contents

Preface

Antique dealer and "conflator thereof," voyeur and narcissist, Bertie Bolger is the intense and amusing protagonist of one of Sean O'Faolain's later stories, "An Inside Outside Complex." He is one of several O'Faolain characters who project the writer's ironical self-awareness. Indeed, Bertie's love affair can serve as metaphoric introduction to O'Faolain's mercurial relationship with his native land.

A middle-aged bachelor, Bertie spies into the living room window of a widowed dressmaker named Maisie, falls in love with her domestic image, woos and weds her, feels betrayed and confined by her actuality in marriage, walks out, returns after a year, and reconciles himself to her in a momentary self-perception: that of his mirrored image peering out of Maisie's living room window.

In over fifty years of writing about the Irish and himself as Irishman, O'Faolain has blended strong impulses of idealization, alienation, and reconciliation. He gazes wistfully through a personal window into his people's world, peers out of that window with equal longing at the non-Irish world, and casts his mirrored image on the glass as self-conscious Irishman and Irish citizen of the world. His large body of fiction, social criticism, cultural analysis, and historical biography harmonizes a native intimacy with a cosmopolitan freedom of mind.

O'Faolain's representative qualities are numerous; to look into his work is to examine the conflicting soul of modern Ireland. Born with the twentieth century, he inherited native shares of poverty, religious orthodoxy, political revolution, and literary idealism as one might ingest a warring combination of drugs. For an artist of his generation, a revulsion-attraction complex over these inheritances was almost inevitable. These artists often considered Ireland "a place or state of punishment," an ignorant and domineering parent, and, at the same time, a "Golden land" dreamed of in their youth, the anchor of all their interests and sympathies.

O'Faolain confronts this Irish conflict of the heart more directly than any other modern Irish writer. That directness, supported by a fearless curiosity, an integrated humanity, and a skillful artistry, makes him an exceptional touchstone for the modern Irish personality.

This study consists of four chapters. The first, "A Life Won for Literature," considers the biographical bases for the evolution of O'Faolain's thought. It discusses formative events, his recollections, and literary recreations of parts of his life. It also scans his publishing career in order to characterize the growth of his literary personality.

"Nationality and Beyond," the second chapter, analyzes the complications of O'Faolain's generational inheritance of literary renaissance and political revolution. It examines how this inheritance (and how particular writers and patriots) affected his work as Irish cultural spokesman and social critic.

The third chapter, "The Spirit of Physical Life," discusses O'Faolain's fictional art, and particularly his creation of character, character crisis, and atmosphere as an extension of and a surrounding for his characters.

The last chapter, "Extensions of Irishness," deals with O'Faolain in the context of modern Irish literature, his representative and unique characteristics as an Irish writer. It suggests similarities in motive and style to the work of a few of his Irish predecessors, contemporaries, and followers.

I thankfully acknowledge the timely support of my home institution for a 1981 Central Connecticut State University research grant. I am very grateful to Sean O'Faolain and his wife Eileen for their kind hospitality and cheerful encouragement when I visited them in 1981, and for his generous permission to quote from his works.

With sorrow at his passing, I recall an old debt of learning to Professor George Brandon Saul, who led me into the green world of modern Irish literature. I thank my dear friend, Professor Victor Kaplan, for stimulating advice during the early stages of composition. Mostly I thank my wife Janice for insight, advice, and years of loving encouragement.

Richard Bonaccorso

CHAPTER ONE

A Life Won for Literature

The decisive elements of Sean O'Faolain's childhood and youth include his parentage, his home life in the city of Cork, the religious and political ambience of the times, his education, his involvement in revolutionary activities, and his travels. These, which make up the greater part of his first thirty years, become significant material in his memory-life and creative career. That career formally begins around his thirtieth year. It is in the published works of the next fifty years that the essential life of the man and artist grows and defines itself.

Sean O'Faolain was born John Whelan on February 22, 1900, in the Irish city of Cork. He was to live there, with holiday and wartime interruptions, for the first twenty-six years of his life. The family, poor but industrious, lived over a pub and then over an electrician's shop on the two ends of Half Moon Street, a short lane striking south from the Lee quays into what Corkmen still call "the flat of the city." Across that narrow, facade-shadowed street was the stage door to the old Cork Opera House. There young John got his first glimpses of touring theatrical people. Most of them were English; most of the performances were subliterary popular entertainments, though they fed the boy's imagination week by week for almost twenty years. Renters of two floors above the electrician's shop, the

Whelans sublet most of the house for weekly lodging, notably to some of the theatre people, a circumstance that O'Faolain recalls with relish.

> . . . a bearded gentleman with a deep voice paused at the kitchen door to have a friendly word with my father, tipped my chin with a smile and passed slowly on.
> "A very nice gentleman," my father said when he was gone. "Very well spoken. He is the ghost of Hamlet's father." Simon Legree helped me every evening for a week with my simple arithmetical problems; he was much more helpful than long John Silver. . . .[1]

He also recalls (in the early pages of his autobiography, *Vive Moi!*) falling in love with an actress who was sawn in two every night by a performer called The Great Lafayette. He was then ten years old. A comic and touching fictionalization of his childhood yearnings is his story "Billy Billee," which tells of a kind of love affair between a fourteen-year-old boy and a fleshy, middle-aged dancer.[2]

The raciness of these associations is hardly typical of those early years, however. Both parents, farm-bred and upright, raised John and his two older brothers by a standard he would remember as oppressive and pathetic.

> We were shabby-genteels at the lowest possible social level, always living on the edge of false shames and stupid affections, caught between honorable amibitions and pathetic fears, between painful strugglings and gallant strivings, never either where we were or where we hoped to be, Janus-faced, throwing glances of desire and admiration upwards and ahead, glances of hatred or contempt downwards and behind.[3]

His mother, the former Bridget Murphy from near Rathkeale in Limerick, was an oppressive pietist in a rigorous Irish-Catholic mold. O'Faolain considers that his feelings for her were ultimately undermined by her "religious melancholy": "As a boy I loved her dearly, as a youth I ceased to love her, as a grown man I pitied her."[4] His father Denis, Queen's County-born, became a humble Cork policeman of the Royal Irish Constabulary, duty-bound to his heart's core. O'Faolain recalls him as a worshipper of the imperial hierarchies, indeed, he thinks of him as a symbol, "the humble but priceless foundation-stuff on which all great states and empires have raised themselves, deviously, to power . . . ."[5] The adverb suggests the mature writer's political sentiments (he considers himself a "natural, if mild rebel"[6]) though as a boy he shared his father's empire patriotism. He would grow increasingly alienated from his father, not as much over political differences as for a missing personal bond. "I feel downcast," he writes, "that I can only remember my father like this as a figure, almost a type, rather than as a person. His own, inner, private life is hidden from me completely."[7]

O'Faolain's home ties loosened in his late teens, unravelled during the revolutionary early 1920s, and finally severed in 1926 when he left Cork to go study in the United States. His fictional and autobiographical recollections of both parents oscillate between surges of love, dismay, respect, pity, and regret. Most often he protrays them as victims of their own ethical rigidity.

"Up the Bare Stairs"[8] is a story which objectifies not an actual event but what he elsewhere calls the "enslaving love" of his childhood home. In that tragicomic tale a boy returns home (the house on Half Moon Street is its model) after being kept late at school. His teacher, knowing the boy will have to explain his punishment to his hard-working parents, is grilling him for not knowing his Euclid and for letting down his class team, named the Mollies after John Redmond's political faction. The father, "one of the hottest Redmondites in the city of Cork," reacts as if his son has committed treason. The mother's response cuts deeper, for, added to the father's, it suggests a degeneration from family uprightness to servility.

" 'Oh, for God's sake Billy,' says the mother, 'don't mind
John Redmond. 'Tis little John Redmond or any other John
Redmond cares about us, but 'tis the work, the work. What
are we slaving for, boy, day and night, and all the rest of it.
There's your poor father working himself to the bone to send
you through school. And so on. Nothing matters, boy, but
the work! The work!'
" 'Tisn't only the work,' says the old man. 'Tisn't only
the work,' and he was sobbing over it. 'But to think of poor
John Redmond fighting night after night for Ireland, standing up there in the House of Commons, and you — you
brat — couldn't even do a sum in Euclid to stand by him! In

3

your own school! Before everybody! Look at him,' he wails, with his arm up to the picture of John Redmond on the wall, with his hooded nose and his jowls like an old countrywoman. 'Look at the dacent gentleman. A man that never let down his side. A gentleman to the tips of his toes if there ever was one. And you couldn't do a simple sum in Euclid to help him. Th'other fellows could do it. The All Fors could do it. But my son couldn't do it!'

"And with that he gave me a crack that nearly sent me into the fire."

On both idealistic and realistic grounds, these parents are pitiful types, projections of the shabby-genteel mentality that afflicted O'Faolain's childhood home, with its pathetic worship of the gentleman and its unhealthy obsession with a joyless and mindless success by work. For the son in the story (Francis Nugent, now a grown man recalling the family scene) this event began to destroy his respect for his parents; he pitied them so much that he felt compelled to succeed, not to please them but to escape from them and their humiliation.

"The end of it was that I was on my knees with my head on the mother's lap, blubbering, and the old man with his two hands up to John Redmond, and the tears flowing down his face like rain, and the mother wailing, 'Won't you promise, Frankie, won't you promise to work, boy,' and I promising and promising anything if she'd only stop crying."[9]

O'Faolain grew up feeling a similar compulsion. It is suggestive of his emotinal resilience, however, that he imbues this scene with a kind of mock-heroic comedy, heightened by the incongruous mixture of nationalist politics and domestic squabbling.

In a more tragic mood, O'Faolain's early fiction often uses the device of alienated father and son to depict the revolutionary evolution of modern Ireland. "The Small Lady,"[10] a long tale of the Black and Tan conflict; *A Nest of Simple Folk*,[11] a novel which culminates with the 1916 Rising; and *Bird Alone*,[12] a novel set in Cork after the death of Parnell, all use father-son disputes to evoke the moral turmoil between Irish generations. These works suggest O'Faolain's troubled relationship with his father when he began to break away from the parental value system. His recreations of his mother turn

4

up more in his later fiction, focusing more on the conflicts of home life than of the public sphere.

In later years he recalls his parents more favorably, though always with a qualification. "The Kitchen,"[13] a late story originally conceived as a passage of autobiography, celebrates his mother's old-age steadfastness to her home, though he sees that home as a useless relic of bygone life. In *Vive Moi!* he remembers a tender reunion with his parents during the Civil War, when he was an Irregular on the run.[14] Though they could not understand or approve of his politics, they remained loyal to him as their son. It is typical of O'Faolain to admit his emotional ties to them even as he speaks of his alienation from their ways.

Perhaps his most pleasant fictionalization of them is his brief story, "The Sugawn Chair."[15] It captures their simple affections and frustrations in a recollection of an autumn day when an annual sack of potatoes and apples was delivered to them, "up from the country." The sack reminds them of their happier days as farm youngsters. For a few hours they put off their acquired restraint and, as the writer declares, fall "madly in love again." To him their sentimental recreations of their farm pasts is a beautiful imposture. Yet, through remembered images of chair and sack, a reverie of Limerick apples, dust, and turf becomes his own, years after his parents are dead.

Though his parents are a basis for much of his fiction, family life is not as important a subject to him as it is in most modern Irish fiction writers. O'Faolain is more concerned with the fate of individuals and individualism within family confines. This differentiates him, for example, from his fellow Corkman, Frank O'Connor, a writer to whom family life has a special inherent value. O'Faolain is a naturally independent soul, and such parents as his must have unwittingly hurried him on his way early in his life. In spite of their ambitions, they probably never considered themselves socially worthy of passionate, individual lives. O'Faolain's whole instinct as a writer is to discover personal passion, particularly in those who keep it hidden. In a 1981 statement about his writing he remarks:

> I at least have had the imagination and the sympathy to guess that every character, in every situation, contains a hidden truth that, if one works hard enough, . . . will reveal

5

itself when the last shred of the conventional disguise falls at the story's end.[16]

The personal, hidden truth can become a dignifying agent when its possessor recognizes it and strives to nurture it in spite of opposition, whether that opposition be institutional, cultural, societal, or familial.

Given Ireland's political heritage, this conflict between the personal and the imposed is evocative of an everlasting Irish identity crisis. When O'Faolain was a boy growing up in Cork, Ireland itself had a hidden truth and an unrealized dignity about it. As a boy he was unaware of this hidden Ireland; as a young man he became obsessed with it. He recalls the land of his birth as

> a place that did not exist . . . . which then was, politically, culturally, and psychologically just not there. All that was there was a bastard piece of the British Empire . . . . I had . . . no consciousness of my country as a separate cultural entity . . . .[17]

His boyhood heroes were fictional and historical Englishmen, and he was as proud as his father was of any Irishman who could establish himself in the English world picture. The experience of his later youth during the Irish rebellion would uncover the internal Irishman to him for the first time, a native being who could be admirable for his own sake.

During his schooldays, British imperialism and Irish Catholicism existed in an odd state of compromise, a rendering unto Caesar of everything but faith and morality. He attended the Irish-Catholic Lancastrian National School, an ill-equipped, antique, dirty, and rough institution. It was staffed by Presentation Brothers, childlike, hard-working souls transplanted from the country. O'Faolain fondly recalls his days there, the underdog cameraderie and the eagerness for learning.

The learning was not always enlightened, however, particularly concerning biological matters. The sexual prudery of Irish-Catholic culture first expressed itself to young John through his teachers and priests. The boys were told, for example, "that circumcision is a small circle cut from the foreheads of Jewish children."[18] Sexuality had no linguistic expression beyond evasive circumlocutions.

6

"Company-keeping" was spoken of in solemn tones. Irish churchmen taught, O'Faolain says,

> as if they had decided that in all such matters as the flesh familiarity breeds desire, or as if they considered that God, in creating desire for woman in man, had been guilty of a lapse of taste about which the least said the better.[19]

In O'Faolain's youth there was a group of influential pietists in Cork who had the trees tarred on their trunks along the mile-long lovers' lane called The Mardyke, this "to prevent lovers from sheltering behind them at night!"[20] In recollection O'Faolain wonders how these puritans expected the poor classes to experience love except under the open sky.[21] The answer seems to be that they were expected either not to love at all or to do so in some arid, harmless form. It appears that poverty was meant to be ignorant and passionless in God-fearing Cork.

Contrary to the plight of poor children the world over, a poor Cork boy's efforts to learn the sexual facts of life were a part of his fundamental struggle. The story called "The Talking Trees"[22] (referring to those same Mardyke trees) is a wonderful evocation of that experience.

> Always near every school, there is a Daisy Bolster—the fast girl whom everybody has heard about and nobody knows. They had all seen her at a distance. Tall, a bit skinny, long legs, dark eyes, lids heavy as the dimmers of a car lamp, prominent white teeth, and her lower lip always gleaming wet. She could be as old as seventeen. Maybe even eighteen. She wore her hair up. Dick told them that he had met her once at the tennis club with four or five other fellows around her and that she had laughed and winked very boldly all the time. Georgie said that he once heard a fellow in school say, "She goes with boys." Gong Gong blubbed that that was true because his sister Jenny told him that a girl named Daisy Bolster had been thrown out of school three years ago for talking to a boy outside the convent gate. At this Georgie flew into a terrible rage.
>
> "You stupid slob!" he roared. "Don't you know yet that when anybody says a boy and a girl are talking to one another it means they're doing you-know-what?"

"I don't know you-know-what," Gong Gong wailed. "What what?"[23]

This recreation of those childhood and adolescent confusions, circumlocutions, and bravado, for all of its local flavor, contains a hint of universal inevitability. It also illustrates the futility of "protective" cultures. Most of O'Faolain's childhood stories are metaphors for the rebellion against such protection.

O'Faolain speaks of his life as a series of emancipations. His flight from his parents' narrow world began, ironically, with the family summer visits to the farming regions where his parents had begun their lives. Mrs. Whelan took her three sons on alternate summers to her own sister's in Rathkeale, Limerick, and to the Curragh-plain region in Kildare and County Dublin to stay with Denis's sister. Young John made these trips from childhood until his mid-teens. His mother would tell the children to "drink it in," convinced that country air was in itself medicinal.[24] What John drank in was much more: a sense of timelessness, of human integrity, and affection for the land itself. These became part of his first truly personal values.

The land around Rathkeale was rough, flat, and reedy, a poor and unspectacular part of forgotten Ireland. But under its "unmistakably pallid sky" and in its silence, the boy sensed "a place breathing its own essence."[25] The vacations in the east, by contrast, provided a sense of vastness and freedom, with its grassy plains rolling with heather under "sky-castles of snowy clouds."[26] Two of O'Faolain's novels, *A Nest of Simple Folk* and *Come Back to Erin*,[27] lovingly memorialize Rathkeale, even while depicting its backwardness. The Curragh region is the setting for two love-reveries, the stories entitled "Love's Young Dream" and "A Touch of Autumn in the Air."[28] Near those same regions flows the River Barrow, the drugged summer-setting for "Lady Lucifer,"[29] a story that debates the pleasant and yet threatening consequences of the Irish longing for rural sanctuary. A Wordsworthian in his sensitivity to landscape, O'Faolain is quite anti-Wordsworthian in his distrust of the passivity induced by beautiful places.

After 1917, when O'Faolain was more fully engaged in seeking his independent life, he found in Gougane Barra in the West Cork mountains all the rich associations that rural Ireland offered. In that Gaeltacht region, Gougane Barra was the antique jewel, a mountain-closed valley with a long, narrow lake (the River Lee's source), complete with a hermit island (St. Finnbarr's retreat). He has written two exceptional stories set in this locale, "The Man Who Invented Sin" and "The Silence of the Valley."[30] In his eighteenth summer, young John went to study Irish in the Gaelic League school nearby, and to be with Eileen Gould, a girl from Cork's Sunday's Well. He had met her in an Irish-language class in the city, making his introductions to his future wife by putting her pigtail braid into an inkwell. At Gougane he also met the colorful locals, including Denis Cronin (Dinny Gougane), who owned a fishing hotel by the lake, and an old peasant couple who were legends in their own time, Tim Buckley and his wife Anastasia (The Tailor and Ansty). The Tailor was the voice of the valley, a folk storyteller who entertained all visitors.[31] One regular visitor was an emotional, unorthodox priest, Father Tim Traynor, who was the model for Frank O'Connor's fictional Father Fogarty, and who appears as the fat priest with all of the Gougane locals in O'Faolain's "The Silence of the Valley."

The other O'Faolain story of Gougane, "The Man Who Invented Sin," opens with a charged recollection.

> In our youth when we used to pour into the mountains to learn Irish, places that were lonely and silent for the rest of the year became full of gaiety during the summer months.[32]

Indeed, it was lonely and silent Ireland that was coming to life, for these young people (students, teachers, writers, and patriots) came, as O'Faolain suggests, in a spirit of self-sacrifice and idealism born out of the 1916 Rising, producing a gaiety he "never experienced before or since."[33] The two Gougane Barra stories are elegies to that joyousness. There, in that idealistic spirit, John Whelan changed his name to its Irish Sean O'Faolain. He and his family have kept it so in tribute to those days.

As a fourteen-year-old, prior to these experiences, he had conceived no idea of a resurgent Ireland. He was then enrolled in the Presentation Brothers' secondary school, learning his lessons by cram and rote. On a January night in 1915, however, he went to a performance at the Cork Opera House and saw something so old and familiar that it awoke his imagination. The setting was a parlor in an Irish country home, inhabited by characters who seemed to be his own country relations.[34] The play was Lennox Robinson's Abbey production of *Patriots*. The experience helped him to realize that

his own world was worthy of artistic recreation. Eight years previously, a very similar experience in the same theatre had influenced Lennox Robinson, when as a young man of County Cork he saw his first
Abbey plays.[35] The Irish Renaissance filtered into the national mind
in this way, providing a sense of tradition for would-be writers. The
figure of James Nugent, Robinson's old Fenian hero in *Patriots*, remained in O'Faolain's mind for almost twenty years, and finally
found reexpression in Leo Foxe-Donnel, the solitary revolutionary
of *A Nest of Simple Folk*.[36]

It was not unusual in those years leading up to the Rising for
nationalistic feeling to be communicated in an aesthetic form. The
idea of a renewed Ireland was part of the literary culture, and
Robinson's play was inspiring on both counts. In *Patriots* the passionate nationalism of James Nugent is ignored by the conservative
common folk he lives among, yet through him Robinson suggests the
possibility of a revitalized native life-urge, a potential for a unique
dignity and destiny in the common Irishman. In works of this sort,
Irish subject matter became more appealing and aesthetically
viable.

When the rising in Dublin occurred in 1916, O'Faolain's first
reaction to the news of the insurrection was not much different from
his father's, a feeling that a few Irishmen were disgracing all of
Ireland before the world. This response was typical of the majority
at the time, but as the rebels held out against the onslaught of the
British Army, and after, when they—mostly young idealists— were
shot "in ones, twos, and threes," he felt his inherited beliefs
disintegrating, and he shed secret tears for the martyrs.[37] As was the
case of many of his countrymen, the Rising did not make him a
rebel, but it opened his mind to rebellious thought.

One of O'Faolain's secondary school teachers, Padriac
O'Domhnaill (an Irish-language instructor), was an Irish Volunteer
and drillmaster to a group of ragtag Cork rebels. O'Faolain admired
him as a forceful personality, though he could not at first understand his politics. But when the student saw the teacher wearing a
lapel pin signifying his ability to converse in Irish, it seemed to
O'Faolain a kind of elegance far-removed from the undisciplined
drilling. He took to studying the language with O'Domhnaill's help.
In the same year, 1917, he made his last summer trip with his
mother to Limerick. During the next year, John Whelan became
Sean O'Faolain; met his future wife, Eileen; made his first Gougane

Barra pilgrimage; entered University College Cork on a scholarship; and became an Irish Volunteer.

He could not know at the time where joining the Volunteers would lead him. He was to be a rank and file IRA man for most of the next six years, momentous times for his country and himself. It was love for his compatriots that led him on from the first, a feeling described in *Vive Moi!*.

> Never will I forget the first day I stood in a field, in a deep glen, somewhere to the southwest of the city, with a score of other raw recruits, being given my first drill by some older student, while along the two hills overlooking the glen other Volunteers stood on the lookout . . . . Ray Kennedy, a lecturer in the Chemistry Department, spoke to us about what we were there for, about the coming fight, about secrecy and loyalty. It was an autumn day of sun and shower, and just as he began to speak to us a faint, gentle sprinkling rain began to fall on us, and then the sun floated out again and sparkled on every leaf and blade of grass as if some invisible presence had passed over us with a lighted taper, binding us together not only in loyalty and friendship but in something dearer still that I am not ashamed to call love.[38]

Though the Republican movement would lose its credibility for him by the end of the Civil War, O'Faolain could never cancel this kind of love in himself. As late as 1963 he would say of that love's essential motive: "I wish to God I could believe in anything as fervently now."[39] The war years would be his first important subject as a writer, not for the events of war but for the conflicting stresses of idealism and disillusionment in the rebel mind.

A Nest of Simple Folk deals with the making of a rebel, and ends with news of his involvement in the Rising of 1916. The first story collection, *Midsummer Night Madness*, deals mainly with the hardships of the Anglo-Irish War and the bitterness of the Civil War. In each book the rebel is a lonely person who is living out of his own emotions, committed to a cause but often questioning its validity. He often resembles O'Faolain himself, grown disillusioned but not disaffected, and ultimately making his rebellious stand on his own emotinal and intellectual terms.

The Anglo-Irish War was more a war of nerves than bullets for O'Faolain and most of the Cork student Volunteers. They participated as messengers, agitators, and spies, and occasionally made a public gesture, such as late in 1920 when O'Faolain stood with Volunteers in an honor guard over the body of Terence MacSwiney, Lord Mayor of Cork. MacSwiney, an organizer of the Cork Volunteers, had died after seventy-four days of hunger strike in London's Brixton Prison.

Of the friendships O'Faolain formed in those days, two were to have literary as well as nationalistic significance: those with Daniel Corkery and Michael O'Donovan (Frank O'Connor). Corkery, twenty-two years older than O'Faolain, was an elementary school teacher in Cork, a dramatist, fiction writer, and patriot (he had been a personal friend of MacSwiney). O'Connor, Corkery's former student, was three years younger than O'Faolain. The two younger men became literary confidants, associates in Volunteer activity, and disciples of Corkery. One of O'Connor's first stories, "Laughter," describes an amateurish ambush carried out by a group of young Volunteers. The narrator is a boyish participant, an ironic representation of O'Connor himself. Among the Volunteers is an Eric Nolan, an impoverished but theatrical young man who wears yellow gloves, carries a walking stick, and smokes a pipe, a pose that both impresses the narrator and confuses the military police, who are suspicious of rougher-looking young men. In a dissertation on Corkery, O'Connor, and O'Faolain, Ione Malloy points out that Eric Nolan is an O'Connor version of young Sean O'Faolain.[40]

Between the truce of 1921 and the outbreak of the Civil War in 1922, O'Faolain became a travelling textbook-salesman. He enjoyed the adventures of primitive trains and hotels through much of Ireland, and dreamed of writing an Irish *Dead Souls*. Still only twenty-one, but sporting a mustache to make him look older, he absorbed a good deal of Irish common life as he canvassed the wilds of Kerry and West Clare, excellent preparation for a short story writer.

The Civil War brought him back to Cork in June, where he joined the rebel Republicans. He was assigned as a bomb-maker in the city, a monotonous duty that became tense when the Free State troops began to close in on Cork. "The Bombshop" is a fictional treatment of those days.

> Even when the work began to pall on them, when they
> began to halt in the middle of it to lounge and smoke in the
> front room, or to peep through the drawn blinds at the

streets, they returned shamefaced with a joke about the Freedom of the City that would one day be conferred on them. And when they did at last confess to one another that they would like to go out into the streets it was a long time before they talked of it as something that might possible be done. When they did they found that only two things prevented them—the danger to themselves and the danger to the Bombshop; they might easily be recognized by a spy and arrested, or, worse still and more likely, they might not be arrested at once but watched as they went back to their lair. So they abandoned the idea, only to return to it again, abandon it again, and return to it and abandon it, until the very thought of the streets tormented them.[41]

This passage contains an early version of a major O'Faolain theme, the conflict between self-restriction brought about by fear and the contrary craving for personal freedom. It is a particularly strong motif in his other war stories, such as "Fugue" and "The Patriot,"[42] and it reemerges in many variations throughout his work. Confining circumstance is rather obvious in "The Bombshop," but more subtle, self-imposed restrictions are also present, as are the deep-seated desires to overcome them. This conflict between caution and anarchic desire is so durable in O'Faolain's writing that it reappears as a major story-pattern in his *Foreign Affairs* collection, published forty-four years after "The Bombshop."

By winter of 1922, the Irregulars, as the Republican forces were called, were outflanked and scattering to the West Cork hills, along with their now-mobile bomb shop, which reestablished itself near Ballyvourney, only a few miles north of Gaugane Barra. The romantic mountains had a poignant effect on the young outlaw. O'Faolain witnessed a few sporadic counter attacks, saw the gradual disintegration of the resistance, and ultimately, like many others of the defeated army, experienced separation and flight through the hills. He builds his story "Fugue" out of that experience, though the action of that piece concerns combatants in the Anglo-Irish War.

Before the struggle in West Cork was over, the twenty-two-year-old O'Faolain was given the executed Erskine Childers's job as Director of Publicity for the First Southern Division of the Republican Army.[43] He returned to Cork city and carried out his acivities while in hiding. Eileen Gould was one of his couriers.

Around the time of the truce, O'Faolain was made Republican

Director of Publicity in Dublin. He felt himself unqualified for such a post, wondered at the forces that had thrust it upon him and at the mad political jockeying of DeValera and the other ranking Republicans. he also felt the ludicrousness of his own war efforts, writing in defense of a republic that did not exist.

A sobered twenty-three, O'Faolain returned to University College Cork as an M.A. student. He renewed his friendship with Frank O'Connor, recently released from a Free State prison where he had been held with other Irregulars. In September of 1924, O'Faolain began a teaching job at a Christian Brothers school in Ennis, County Clare, an out-of-the-way situation with limited potential. He remembered Ennis sixteen years later without antagonism, however, in *An Irish Journey.*

> I find that I have nothing but good to say of my experience
> of Ennis and Clare. I spent there one of the happiest years
> of my life. And yet, I had no pastimes but to walk about
> Clare Abbey, and Quin Abbey, and down by Dromoland, or
> even as far as Newmarket-on-Fergus and out over the bog,
> or swim in the river in summer, and study in the winter. But
> then I recall the bank clerks in the Munster and Leinster
> bank whom I used to see walk out the road every evening, in
> a silent group of three, and I think myself back there *in
> perpetuum*, on a small salary . . . .[44]

It was easy, outback Irish life with slowly gathering frustrations, one that O'Faolain depicts in several stories ("A Letter"[45] and "Falling Rocks, Narrowing Road, Cul-de-sac, Stop"[46] are examples). In Ennis he tried to keep up with the outside world by subscribing to literary and social journals, reading about books, plays, and events that were beyond his reach. At the same time, Eileen Gould was also teaching, with even less satisfaction, up in Ballinasloe in East Galway. By spring of 1925, both resigned their jobs, O'Faolain returning to Cork that autumn for a second master's degree and Eileen landing a more substantial teaching post in Naas, near Dublin. O'Connor left Cork at about the same time for a library job in Wicklow. These three, like other young intellectuals in post-revolutionary Ireland, were seeking passage in an Irish lifestream that was neither deep nor swift.

Adding to his feeling of stagnation and isolation, O'Faolain had a falling out with Corkery over political matters. The older writer persisted in a hard-line Republicanism at a time when O'Faolain was feeling his greatest disillusionment with those politics. He was more alone in Cork than ever, but began his true apprenticeship as a creative writer, working out of a rebellious yet elegaic mood. Cork was becoming (to use two of his early expressions) a narrow-minded "Lilliput" and yet a lovely "city-under-the-sea" of reverie. His early writing was an attempt to define and yet overcome Cork's restrictiveness. As a person, he would escape it by means of writing, his study, and personal relationships unconnected with politics. In the following year he would actually leave Cork and Ireland, beginning a period of considerable travel.

Through the good offices of O'Connor, O'Faolain submitted a Cork story, "Lilliput,"[47] to George Russell (AE), who was editor of the *Irish Statesman*. It appeared in that journal on February 6, 1926. Later that year, with the recommendations of AE and Lennox Robinson supporting his bid, he won a Harkness Commonwealth Fellowship to take two years of graduate study in the United States. These were momentous events for him, though he was more thrilled with the publication of his story than with the fellowship. His comments in *Vive Moi!* in recollection of his reaction to the award give an idea of what kind of liberation he still lacked. He tells how he hesitated at his good fortune, introverted and almost overcome by a sentiment that his creativity needed protection from intellectual rigor in an alien environment.

> Remembering my first eager essay into the public world, as a Cephalopod of the I.R.A., and my shocked disillusion after it, I can now better understand this note of caution, though it also frightens and disgusts me that I ever nourished it. Disillusion, caution, skepticism, cynicism, sentimentality—the descent is all too easy into a cowardly softness.[48]

O'Faolain was able to avoid the worst consequences of this caution by making his developing intellect an ally to his maturing imagination. His American experience (he chose to attend Harvard) would help to develop his sense of himself as a world citizen, resulting in a confidence that would give his writing more authority. He would

15

make Ireland his home again afterwards, but never again would Ireland be his only point of reference.

The fellowship was the occasion of his final separation from life in his parents' home. Unaware of this consequence, they were more delighted with the fellowship than he was. He was becoming in their minds the Gentleman they had dreamed he might be. O'Faolain recalls outfitting himself with his mother's help.

> I sent her off after visiting cards, dress shirts with American-style collars attached, a special and hitherto unheard-of kind of expanding cuff link, patent-leather pumps, silk under-trunks, riding gloves with cord-woven palms, white woolen socks for squash, Ascot-type cravats for wearing with my dressing gown at breakfast. She was both shocked and en-chanted by my needs.[49]

The self-ironic comedy of these theatrics continues in his recollec-tion of his father's response.

> I think my father touched the peak of his pride in me the day I told him, rather sheepishly, that I had been summon-ed to London, with all other Fellows, to be presented in St. James's Palace to His Royal Highness the Prince of Wales, later King Edward VIII, now the Duke of Windsor, at the time the patron of the Commonwealth Fund.[50]

It was an odd ceremony for an ex-I.R.A. revolutionary. Yet, in recollection O'Faolain smiles less at the ceremony than at himself.

He spent the next three years in the United States, followed by a period of teaching in England. It would be seven years before he would take up permanent residence in Ireland. While living in Boston and studying at Harvard, he began to write about Ireland with greater intensity, though he was unsure if he would ever return there. Separation gave him a perspective, and travel across the North American continent helped him to decide on his future life in Ireland.

In a travel book published in 1953, *An Autumn in Italy*, O'Faolain (by then a seasoned traveller) muses that for him travel is never a mere "going from one place to another," that it "is never an escape."[51] It always involves self-search, particularly for new dimen-

16

sions in himself. "How different am I capable of being?" he asks himself in *Autumn in Italy*.[52] His American travels in 1926 were as internal as they were geographical.

O'Faolain studied philology at Harvard under the rigorous George Lyman Kittredge regime, admired the scholarly style but felt an aversion to the more mechanical approaches to aesthetic experience. Compromising with his student life, he grew a scholar's beard and maintained A grades, but he also devoted more time to his creative writing than ever before. In 1927, he began to compose the story "Fugue" and part of the novel, *A Nest of Simple Folk*, both works steeped in the passions of the Irish Troubles. He was quite comfortable in Boston, both in Cambridge and the South End, where he sometimes helped friends who ran an immigrants' settlement house. He was fascinated by Boston's old European quality and its new ethnic energy. That city appears several times in his fiction. One re-creation, over fifty years after he first lived there, is in his novel *And Again?*

> I liked its ingrown ways and open spaces, its empty harbour,
> its decayed railroad precincts, its lake-wide river drawing
> after it an endless parade of clouds over parks, ponds, fens,
> reclaimed marshlands . . . , greenery underfoot and
> overhead, hints of monumental boulevards . . . . Nobody
> will ever call Boston exciting or anticipate newness there. On
> the contrary, like Dublin, of which it occasionally and pain-
> fully reminded me, it has the almost untouchable, smellable,
> visible character that comes with a local tradition stubbornly
> maintained . . . .[53]

But Boston was also a place in which to be young. It became his home in a truer sense in the autumn of 1927 when Eileen joined him there; they were married the next June, and in happy-go-lucky style set off on a cross-country camping honeymoon.

Outside Taos, New Mexico, they decided that they would return to Ireland. Taos will always be associated with another artistic traveller, D.H. Lawrence, and a comparison of their responses to the place is revealing. Lawrence spoke of New Mexico's vast deserts and mesas as a great experience for him, a liberation from a European civilization he was tired of, a magnificent experience of a vast and inhuman power.[54] O'Faolain, a more gregarious, less moralistic soul, saw in the same empty spaces a creative alienation, an aesthetic desert.

> . . . could we live in this country always? As we talked I sud-
> denly became aware that, by a trick of light, a last cut-off
> peak seemed to stand up bare and quite alone across the
> plateau beneath us. The vast range had otherwise withdrawn
> itself like mountains in a vision; there was not a soul in
> sight; the dusk was absolutely silent. Even we were oppressed
> by the silence and ceased talking. There wasn't even the
> least cry of a bird. It was an immeasurable night. And it
> wasn't in the least bit impressive—because if those moun-
> tains had associations we did not know them; if history—that
> is, if some sort of purposeful life, other than that of mis-
> sionaries and explorers, ever trod this vastness—it left no
> vibrations for either of us.[55]

For a Lawrence, liberation meant escaping from cultural origins that had overdefined his early existence. For an O'Faolain, libera-
tion meant creating a culture out of the undefined raw material of the Ireland he knew, or at least creating as an artist can, by defining and describing, and showing how life can be lived within the image rendered. What O'Faolain the writer requires of a place is a cultural dimension. He likes to look at, then through, surfaces, wondering how and why the reputation of a place or a people was created. Unlike Lawrence, he is charmed by surfaces, though surfaces are for him a fascination mainly for what they hide.[56] His short-story methodology is directly involved in this uncovering process. In the short story even more than the novel, a surface has to be established, a recognizable image of life from which to curve the story into revelation. At least this is so in the short story as developed by the nineteenth-century European masters and carried forward by O'Faolain, O'Connor, and other modern Irish writers.

The surface was for O'Faolain very Irish; the curve was both Irish and universal. As he indicates in *Vive Moi!* he had, without realizing it at first, established his "fated field."

> By the end of the Civil War life had presented itself to me,
> forever, under the form of a number of ineluctable
> challenges, or experiences, densely compressed into one
> word, Ireland . . . . I might and did look for and find

analogies elsewhere, trying to universalize the data I had in my body experienced locally, but the original data remained. We all make only one basic experiment with life. Everything else is tangential to it. I am impaled on one green corner of the universe.[57]

The O'Faolains returned to Boston for the winter of 1928 as a preparation for their return to Ireland.

They lived in enthusiastic poverty in a chilly apartment off Brattle Street in Cambridge. Eileen taught school from September to June, and Sean completed his M.A. at Harvard. He also taught a course in Anglo-Irish literature at Boston College, published an edition of Thomas Moore lyrics,[58] began some translations of Gaelic poetry that would become part of *The Silver Branch*,[59] and published his story "Fugue" in Harvard's *Hound and Horn*.[60] That tale of fear, flight, and loneliness was a fresh expression of the Irish revolutionary experience. It is full of clashing moods of violence and yearning matched by impressive depictions of blustering weather in panoramic landscapes. These are qualities that can also be found in Corkery's fiction. O'Faolain was still under his elder's influence, yet the story has his own youthfulness and subtlety in it, and it is an advance in Irish writing.

He sent a copy of "Fugue" to Edward Garnett, the London publisher's reader, who replied with a simple but powerful compliment: "You are a writer."[61] It was the kind of encouragement that O'Faolain needed. Garnett was a grand old literary warrior, and his friendship became vital to O'Faolain during the period of his fictional and then physical return to a not-so-hospitable Ireland. Garnett believed in the isolation of an artist in his work, and he scorned the usual measures of success and popularity. He had urged young Liam O'Flaherty to go back to Ireland a few years earlier to write honestly about the peasant world he knew. O'Faolain had already begun his mental journey back to Ireland and into himself. He had armed himself with the confidence of his American experience. Now from London came Garnett's praise and challenge, capping O'Faolain's apprentice years.

The O'Faolains returned to Cork for the summer of 1929, then took up residence outside London at Richmond that autumn. Sean did some teaching at Strawberry Hill, a teacher's college, and worked on the stories that would make up most of his first collection, *Midsummer Night Madness*.

Romantic yet ironic, *Midsummer Night Madness* is an impressive group of tales about the Troubles. Reviewers were enthusiastic. One, the writer L.A.G. Strong, commented in *The Spectator* on O'Faolain's power of suggestion and range of emotion, particularly in the "rich and extraordinary" title story.[62] The book was to have its problems with the censors in Ireland, however. Garnett seemed to anticipate them in the Foreward, written in the cantankerous style of his attacks on English bad taste. This time, however, he took on an Irish lack of taste, a cultural apathy.

> It is time that the Irish people were aware that a nation that
> takes so little interest in its own writers and leaves them
> dependent on English attention and English alms is cultural-
> ly speaking contemptible . . . . I write this as an Anglo-
> Irishman . . . who has always taken an interest in Irish
> authors and Irish literature.[63]

Garnett writes with an insider's anger (his mother was Irish), mainly directed at Daniel Corkery's recently published *Synge and Anglo-Irish Literature*; Corkery had disclaimed Anglo-Irish literature as a national literature, and furthermore had branded it as an alien, expatriate body of writing, seeking a foreign critical approval. Corkery would certainly consider Garnett's involvement with Irish writers a foreign interference. In the Foreward, Garnett blames the intellectual alienation on the parochialism of Ireland, not on its writers, and praises O'Faolain as one who properly asserts his Irishness, that is, as a universalist.

The suggestion (encouraged by Corkery) that Irishness somehow excluded universal concerns was at the heart of the Irish censorship question. Censorship in Ireland was to a large degree a tool for those who feared foreign cultural domination. They saw outside influences as threats to Irish integrity, and they expressed themselves as moral puritans while espousing Irish exclusivism. *Midsummer Night Madness* was banned by the Irish Censorship Board as obscene. There are a number of thoughtful treatments of sexual desire in the book, including an adulterous affair in "The Small Lady," but there is nothing to justify the obscenity judgement. Of course, the Board never did have to justify its decisions. O'Faolain records: "Outwardly I laughed at the news. In my heart I felt infuriated and humiliated."[64] Like the political problems of the Ireland of his youth, this moral-cultural issue became personal; it would directly preoccupy him for the next fifteen years and indirectly be involved with his writing from 1932 on. But every conflict taken on involves a turning away from others. The book was humorously dedicated to Eileen as "this firstling, because from Politics, America, and Scholarship, thou has delivered us!" Personal relationships tended to lead him into and out of public involvements. The O'Faolains returned to Ireland with their newborn child, Julia, in June 1933. Ireland would be their permanent home, though they now belonged to a larger world. They moved into a house near Glencree in the Wicklow Hills, not very far from what Frank O'Connor considered a necessary precaution for Irish writers, the mail boat.

Prior to returning, O'Faolain had pursued the post of professor of English at University College Cork; it was given to Corkery instead. That job would have given him a secure living in Ireland, but he later felt that it would not have suited him for long. He took on the economically precarious life of a freelance writer. While finishing his novel *A Nest of Simple Folk*, he became a regular essayist and reviewer in *Spectator, New Statesman,* and other journals.

He became a founder-member of the Irish Academy of Letters, a literary group of still-lively elders led by the ageing Yeats. The Academy was a formal link for O'Faolain to some of the great people of the Irish Renaissance, though physically that connection only amounted to a few banquet nights spent in the company of Yeats, Gogarty, Lord Dunsany, and others. He was witnessing the passing of Dublin's great literary period, and he knew it, recording that he felt "a tide receding about me."[65]

He renewed his friendship with Frank O'Connor again, this time in the more extroverted world of Dublin. Though they were quite different in temperament, fate had treated them similarly, and they supported each other in controversy and creative struggle. Some of their stories have such a similarity in tone that they could pass for each other's. The urban, lower middle-class tales often have this likeness, particularly those set in their native Cork. Of their conscious role in Irish letters, O'Faolain says that they "chose to imagine that the responsibility for the future of Irish Literature was on our two backs."[66] That they should feel this way (it was not far from

21

fact) could be partially attributed to Yeats's influence, for the great poet had said to O'Connor, "You will save the Abbey Theatre, and O'Faolain will save the Academy."[67] They were destined instead to give voice to the hitherto silent Ireland of Catholic, urban, unheroic, middle-class life.

The 1930s were productive years for O'Faolain. His work during the decade suggests a struggle through his cultural and psychological inheritance toward a more personal perspective. *A Nest of Simple Folk* (a title variation from Turgenev) was for O'Faolain a conjuring of his voiceless childhood and roots. The novel begins in Limerick in 1854 and ends in Cork in 1916, moving out of a time of silence into one of dissonance. In reviewing the book, Graham Greene pointed to the importance of place as a unifier of the novel's various moods.[68] The flat fields around Rathkeale are evoked in a mesmeric manner.

> The two sisters had drunk in the essence of that place, walking along and along in their youth by the toppling riverbanks of the Deel where it flowed beside them with muted strings; along and along, facing the distant church tower whose grey finger of silence rose faintly on the absolutely level horizon.[69]

It is this poetry of stillness that informs the character of Leo Foxe-Donnel, the novel's revolutionary protagonist. Under his rebelliousness is a peasant patience and doggedness that can wait out the years with an unwavering purpose. Yet he is also a person of huge arrogance, having tasted privilege in his childhood. He is underground-Ireland resurgent, not just against the foreign oppressor but also against the moral constraints of the Irish community. He is the first of O'Faolain's subversive heroes; each of his first three novels has one for a protagonist.

In his youth, before he becomes a Fenian, Leo is a threat to all virginity in the countryside. He carries his lechery like a grudge, and it inevitably transmutes into revolutionary fervor. As he grows older, he seems more subdued, yet he remains a sexual and social aberrant, a brooding, anarchic presence to his community. He is the second of a sequence of old or ageing lechers in O'Faolain's early fiction, the first being old Henn, the ragged aristocrat of "Midsummer Night Madness."[70] A third example of this type is another Fenian, old Philip Crone of O'Faolain's second novel, *Bird Alone*. Perhaps this kind of characterization is a Yeatsian influence, a Hanrahan fixation suggesting romantic relationships between sexual, imaginative, and political freedom. The sexual dimension is a significant element in O'Faolain's characterizations (something missing in much of Irish fiction before O'Faolain). His people, early and late, young and old, heroic and unheroic, respond to sexual needs; the manners of their responses are measures of their honesty and humanity.

Though the heroes of O'Faolain's first three novels are in various ways subversive and opposed to the social majority, they all ultimately reveal by their fates the individual's need for a social life of some meaning. Leo Foxe-Donnel finds a kind of salvation in becoming a Fenian, and crowns his life by taking part in the 1916 Rising, though by then he is an old man.

The revolutionary period of O'Faolain's youth had been the creation of extroverts who often displayed their individuality on the grand scale. But post-revolutionary Ireland had become painfully introverted, zenophobic, and suspicious of native dissent. O'Faolain's first serious biography (he had tried an idealistic gloss on DeValera in 1933,[71] a subject he reworked six years later in an analytic style[72]) was *Constance Markievicz*, which he published in 1934.[73] One of the most flamboyant of the 1916 rebels, Constance Goore-Booth (Countess Markievicz) was an extreme model of the extroverted romantic revolutionary. O'Faolain dubs her "an incurable diletante" and adds that "the only art she excelled in was the art of living."[74] Yet, the book is a profoundly sympathetic portrait. For the writer looking back at the period and at such a figure, the biography is an objectification of the Irish political romanticism that swept him up in his youth. The study contains a series of mini-biographies of notable people of the revolutionary generation. This rational look at contemporary Ireland's irrational inheritance is tonally significant. The romantic past was becoming the sentimental property of mundane, establishment Ireland; in *Constance Markievicz*, O'Faolain helps to rescue the heroic generation from sentimental devaluation.

O'Faolain was not only trying to understand his own obsessions; he was beginning in the 1930s to extend his sympathies into various corners of Irish life that were less his own. The Markievicz biography begins with a look at the inner stresses of Anglo-Irish aristocratic life in Dublin at the beginning of the century. O'Faolain is just as interested in Markievicz's social class and its comedies as in her political career and its tragedies. The comedy is serious to him. Her apparent contradictions, though often treated cynically by others, are part of her dignity to O'Faolain, for she is to him a historical example of a soul struggling against the bounds of inherited identity. This is his great fictional theme; it is this kind of character (in all social classes) that would amuse, fascinate, and inspire him always.

In its flamboyant subject, *Constance Markievicz* is in keeping with his tendency toward larger-than-life characters in his earliest fiction. But in *Bird Alone*, the second novel, and in *A Purse of Coppers*,[75] the second story collection, O'Faolain makes significant progress as a characterizer of common humanity. By doing so, he creates a more modern fictional world. I have suggested that an important aspect of O'Faolain's characters is their sexuality. His common folk have sexual desires, often submerged within them as they conform to the moral order by their overt behavior. For these people, sex is sublimated, denied, consciously repressed, or devalued rather than released in bodily fulfillment. A few consciously struggle against the sexual repressions of their society.

Corney Crone, the protagonist of *Bird Alone*, becomes a pariah in his city, Cork, for making the girl he loves pregnant, a fate she is so ashamed of that it drives her to suicide. O'Faolain does not make Corney a hero for giving way to his natural and commonplace desires. But he is worthy of a good deal of sympathy for the tragedy he suffers and of some admiration for his refusal after the tragedy to publically repent.

In *A Purse of Coppers* there are two stories that contain themes of denied or punished sexuality in a puritanical culture. Essentially comic-satiric, "The Old Master" is set in Cork city; the more sombre "Kitty the Wren" is set in Connemara. "The Old Master" introduces a countertype to the ageing lecher: the ageing celibate. John Aloysius Gonzaga O'Sullivan, a rotund would-be man-of-the-world, is condemned to live timidly as a Cork law-librarian. A visit of the Russian Ballet is his undoing, for in becoming associated with the dancers, whom he idolizes, he exposes himself to the vengeance of the church-militant, the Men of St. Mark who march under a banner which blares: "DOWN WITH IMMORAL PLAYS!" John Aloysius is so terrified by this confrontation that he hides in a public privy, catches a chill there, and later dies of it. The high sexuality of art, which O'Sullivan worships as a safe outlet for his buried passions, ultimately forces him to confront his truth, symbolized by the public privy, the debased hiding place for his sexual life.

"Kitty and Wren" tells of an ostracized woman of the glens who lives a purgatorial existence with a mad brother as a community punishment for a love affair ten years past. A French sailor on shore liberty, seeking a loose woman, hears vague gossip of her and travels out to her bogland cabin. He is both delighted and horrified by the woman he finds, delighted by her obvioius hunger for life and horrified by her complete acceptance of her punishment. Though most of *A Purse of Coppers* is grim in tone and mindful, as George Brandon Saul has noted, of Joyce's *Dubliners*, [76] there is a spark of personality in each downtrodden character. In the author, as Graham Greene observes in a review of the collection, there is an "immense creative humour."[77] O'Faolain seems disillusioned but not despairing.

He shows more of a comic vision as he matures, thanks to his ability to analyze his own obsessions in a detached manner. And though his writing was controversial and combative during the 1930s, he was also developing a private and durable perspective from which to view Irish life. A public participant, he was not a public creature. The range of his publications in 1938 and 1939 is indicative of his growing confidence in handling a wide spectrum of Irish subject matter. Within these two years, his one play, a farce entitled *She Had to Do Something*,[78] was produced at the Abbey Theatre; he completed and published *The Silver Branch*, an edition of translations, several by himself, of old Irish poetry; he published what is generally considered his finest biography, *King of the Beggars*,[79] a life of Daniel O'Connell; and he wrote a second, more studious and critical biography of Eamon DeValera, entitled *DeValera*.

The play, reminiscent of his story "The Old Master" in its situation, is an allegory on the relationship between art and the Church in modern Ireland. O'Faolain prefaced the published version causually.

In this comedy a lively Frenchwoman marooned in Ireland in a provincial town finds life deadly dull, strangled by inhibitions. Her efforts to live fully under these adverse conditions make, in a tragi-comic way, the general contrast between Poetry and Puritanism.[80]

There is nothing casual, however, about O'Faolain's concern for this subject matter. Yet, still a young writer, he was able to make of that concern a farce on Irish manners, or the lack of them, ending up with an extroverted creation suggestive of a cross between Oscar Wilde and Paul Vincent Carroll. The stage was not O'Faolain's *metier*, though he joined the immortals of the Abbey on opening night when he took his curtain bows to "a storm of boos and hisses."[81]

By contrast, *The Silver Branch*, though far from rhapsodic in its assessment of old Irish verse, is a labor of cultural piety. The two biographies, of O'Connell and DeValera, are by their subjects and their handling opposite to each other. O'Faolain portrays O'Connell as a man of the world, a European, and a pragmatist forced by circumstances within and around him into idealistic leadership. He protrays DeValera as a man imbued with his humble beginnings, an Irish introvert, and an idealist forced by history into pragmatist politics. O'Faolain greatly admires the tolerant, broad-minded O'Connell type of Irish leader, yet praises DeValera as, at his best, a tremendous symbol of independence and honesty to the common Irishman. He is severely critical of DeValera's practical leadership.

Like Yeats before him, O'Faolain, though a man of strong opinion, was able to find value in interesting personalities, despite antipathy to their ideologies. In an essay on AE published in 1937, he makes a qualifying statement about an artist's kind of belief: ". . . there is only one kind of heterodoxy valuable to a man of letters, and that is the denial of his own self-made faith, the clash between his secret selves."[82] O'Faolain values his ability to understand life's complexity and variety more than his ability to make ultimate judgements.

1940 was a significant year in O'Faolain's creative life. He published a novel, *Come Back to Erin*, something he would not do again for almost forty years; he published a travel book on Ireland, *An Irish Journey*, a beautiful evocation of small-town imagery and culture; and he originated a new magazine, *The Bell*, of which he would be editor for over six years.

The Bell became one of the finest literary and cultural magazines of its time, its editor taking on a heavy literary and social responsibility. He provided a haven of encouragement for a generation of young Irish writers suffering from anti-intellectualism at home and, because of Irish neutrality during the war, dire marketing consequences abroad. O'Faolain became personally involved in launching careers. Among those whose youthful work appeared in *The Bell* were Brendan Behan, Anthony C. West, Michael McLaverty, James Plunkett, Bryan MacMahon, John Montague, and Michael Farrell. It was also a medium for the more established, including Frank O'Connor, Brinsley Macnamara, Lennox Robinson, Patrick Kavanagh, Elizabeth Bowen, Liam O'Flaherty, and Peadar O'Donnell, who succeeded O'Faolain as editor in 1946. As literary editor, O'Faolain called for unornamented visions of Irish reality, not Irish dreams, and he invited his readers to become writers, to take part in expressing their country's actual, not traditional, symbols.

> You know a turn of the road, an old gateway somewhere, a well-field, a street corner, a wood, a handful of quiet life, a triangle of sea and rock, something that means Ireland to you. Men and women who have suffered or died in the name of Ireland, who have thereby died for Life as they know it, have died for some old gateway, some old thistled lagfield in which their hearts have been stuck since they were children.[83]

He believed that what is well-known is well-loved and therefore symbolic of the Irish identity as it is felt, not merely as it is taught.

For O'Faolain, *The Bell* was a celebration and a criticism of the real; for its readers, it was an imaginative liberation. Such an editorship required courage, tedious labor, and patience. Dermot Foley, a librarian living in Ennis in those days, recalls seeking out this literary leader named O'Faolain in his Parkgate Street office in Dublin.

> I found him in a tiny room with a pile of manuscripts, mostly in longhand. As well as I can recall, he put three or four to one side after a while, and groaned. "A few seeds in that lot," he said. "Question is, will I ever get them to sprout?"[84]

O'Faolian never entirely turned away from his early teacher's trade, though the students and the purpose often changed. In *The Bell* the country was his classroom. About two thousand copies per issue made their way into the country, and about one thousand abroad.[85]

He became known as a penetrating social critic and cultural commentator. Almost single-handedly he took on the shibboleths of Gaelic exclusivism and literary censorship. In later years, when asked by his daughter Julia about the attacks on his editorial positions and whether he felt alienated by them, he answered: "Not at all. No. In the days of *The Bell* I was fully integrated because I was on the attack. I had accepted responsibility as a citizen . . . . "[86] The private man had again gone public for his country, but on his own terms. A few of the titles of his editorials give an idea of his battles: "Provincialism," "The Senate and Censorship," "Gaelic—The Truth," "That Typical Irishman," and "The Pleasures and Pains of Ireland."

O'Faolain's friendship with O'Connor deteriorated during the *Bell* years. One sore point was O'Connor's distrust of O'Faolain's man-of-the-world poise. O'Connor's sensibility was built upon a rejection of public for private relationships, and though he craved public approval, he often inspired the opposite because of his irascibility. O'Faolain, on the other hand, thought it a part of self-possession to test his personal integrity in public confrontation, did not oppose institutions merely because they existed, and was cool, convincing, and rather successful under fire. He recognized and accepted their differences easier that O'Connor could, speaking of "Mick and I" in characterizing their temperamental opposition. They would continue to support each other in social controversies and to praise each other as writers. But in the 1940s they felt themselves parting toward separate ends as writers and individuals, and would meet as friends only occasionally in middle age. By the mid 1950s they were avoiding each other. O'Faolain speaks of their alienation as a "mutual loss,"[87] and in later years praises O'Connor's "fantastical gifts" and "wide humanity."[88] In the 1950s, when the friendship was over, O'Connor would call O'Faolain "the one great writer" living in Ireland.[89]

In 1946, O'Faolain stepped down as editor in order to devote more time to his own writing. Peadar O'Donnell, who had been managing editor, took over the formal editorship, with O'Faolain continuing as book editor and occasional contributor. He left his

28

post with a touch of battle fatigue, surprised at his growing detachment from the many fights he had waged with "bourgeoisie, Little Irelanders, chauvinists, puritans, stuffed-shirts, pietists, Tartuffes, Anglophobes, Celtophiles . . . ."[90] That detachment would have a positive effect on his story writing, however, for he would create some of his finest during the next few years, often populating them with individualized versions of the types he had attacked as editor.

He was not done as public Irishman. During the mid-1940s he became founder of an artist's trade union and Vice President of Irish Civil Liberties. At the end of the decade he would publish a cultural history of his country, an even-tempered but spritely criticism of Irish strengths and weaknesses through the ages.

That study, *The Irish*,[91] mythologizes Irish cultural history as a struggle with its own incompleteness, a theme which directly challenges the nationalistic myth of self-sufficiency. The book is not a devaluation of Irish heritage, however, but rather a forward-looking reinterpretation. O'Faolain sees the native instinct as tending toward the extravagantly imaginative, unique, energetic, but lacking in direction. Yet, just as essential a part of Irish heritage is an opposite tendency toward foreign assimilation, a native adaptation to foreign techniques for living, not gained by conquest but in fact by being conquered. Ireland's invaders (and in O'Faolain's mythic context, Christianity is itself one of the invaders) brought their cruelties, divisive influences, and restrictions, but they also left "gifts," influences that would instigate Irish awareness of Irish potential. This learning process would help Ireland to evolve toward a more tolerant, tasteful, and European culture, without alienating itself from the best aspects of its native instinct, particularly its immemorial craving for freedom. It is no mere coincidence that many of O'Faolain's fictional characterizations display a similar line of development, a liberation from an excessive internalization to a more worldly accomodation. *The Irish* concludes with a series of chapters on Irish types and cultural groups (peasants, Anglo-Irish, rebels, priests, writers, politicians), tracing the condition of modern Irish sensibility through them.

The Irish is a unique book: imaginative, rational, critical, and constructive. It seems a serious development off of a less-serious Irish genre, the mythic tour guide. Liam O'Flaherty's very funny diatribe on Irish corruptions, *A Tourist's Guide to Ireland*,[92] may be a quirky parent to *The Irish*. O'Flaherty singles out priests, politicians, publicans, and peasants for his satire. *The Irish* is not at all satiric, nor does it seek to make moral points about Irish virtue and vice. It *does* counter a number of sentimental Irish conceptions about the glories of ancient and early Christian Ireland, and about an exclusively native culture.

The Irish takes up the same controversial issues that O'Faolain fought over in the pages of *The Bell*; yet, as a cultural history it displays a greater sense of distance and tonal calm. The stories that he was writing in the same period also have the mellowness of distance about them. *Teresa and Other Stories* (*The Man Who Invented Sin* in American edition) contains some of O'Faolain's most clear-minded, humorous, and yet beautiful evocations of Irish life. This is the collection that includes "The Man Who Invented Sin," "The Silence of the Valley," and in the American edition, "Up the Bare Stairs," each a masterpiece in counterpointing moods of satire and elegy. O'Faolain was finding that he was not by nature a pure satirist, but more of an ironic romantic.

This tonal mixture is very Chekhovian, for to paraphrase O'Faolain on the Russian master and to apply the paraphrase to himself, he can condemn even while writing with great sensitivity of the thing condemned.[93] A passage from "Lady Lucifer" of the same collection is illustrative. Three friends—doctor, priest, and bank clerk—are poling down the still waters of the River Barrow in County Kildare.

> "If somebody gave me that house and a job as lock-keeper
> I'd be happy for ever after."
> The clerk was only a bank-clerk by avocation: his inward life was in his writing; he wrote novels and stories, over the name of Malachy Lucas. The priest agreed with him, rolling over heavily on his belly, pulling a strand of hay to smell it, murmuring, "Yes—away from everything."[94]

A reader who is aware of O'Faolain's usual handling of this sanctuary theme will not allow himself to be seduced by the drugged atmosphere that the author creates. The passage continues:

> It is a lost corner, barely coming to life, some dim noise
> half-heard through sleep, a moth on a window-pane at mor-

ning, an occasional barge slowly dud-dudding along the river, disturbing the coots and the wild flowers with its arrowy wake. The very air of this deep valley seems too heavy to move. Even then a little cloud lay on the tip of the far line of mountains, too exhausted to persist. The doctor threw a plum-stone into the water. A heron rose from an island and flapped away in bored sloth into the woods.

"You'd have to live on your innards. There's nobody to talk to for miles around. I know I couldn't do it. It's a pipe-dream. And think of the winter nights."

"I can see it at night with my fire and my lamp lighting and not a sound but the rain pocking the canal. A barge nosing the water like an otter. Like an otter. Greasily. Almost silently."

"It's a pipe-dream. The river rises six feet in winter and turns this place into a lake. You'd go crackers."[95]

The theme, strategy, and tonal quality of "Lady Lucifer" owes something to "Gooseberries," a Chekhov story that O'Faolain praises highly. In his delicate way, O'Faolain takes part in the debate on the side of the skeptical doctor, even while evoking the charm that Lucas feels. Both characters represent Irish types, Lucas the hermit (poetic introvert) and the doctor the adventurer (active world-seeker). Both are part of O'Faolain's own makeup. His conscious share in each type is qualified by his knowledge of the other. He decides in the doctor's favor, but shows that his decision is not an easy one.

This maturity of perspective and style has some connection to O'Faolain's travels during the late 1940s into postwar Italy. To use his own words, he recalls that time and experience as part of his "coming of age."[96] The two travel books that resulted from these journeys (*A Summer in Italy*[97] and *An Autumn in Italy*) are evocations of his own temperament in a state of expansion. A greater confidence is evident in all of his works of the 1950s.

The Italian technique for living, relaxed in its coexistence with art, nature, and religion, gave him confidence in instincts he had nurtured within himself in the less compatible Irish environment. He found in the Catholicism of Italy a less suspicious, fearful, and sectarian version of his faith, so congenial at the time that he ironically recalls the experience as an abandonment of the "faith of my fathers" and a conversion to "Roman Catholicism."[98] There is a play on words here, with the small-f "faith" indicating an odd sort of religion (Irish), with the word "fathers" (his pious parents), and on "Roman" (the life-loving city where his "conversion" took place). That event is comically treated in *A Summer in Italy*.[99] O'Faolain's comedy of Italian life emanates out of a lyricism that is partially Italian and partially his own. Walking through fair day in Verona, for example, O'Faolain remarks: "In all this I was making that bridge, which every artist longs for, between the loneliness of his private dreams and the gaiety of the public square."[100]

The relaxed, gregarious, humorous, and expansive aspect of O'Faolain's writing is more than just a style adjustment dating from the 1940s. It is an expression of an essential pursuit of happiness within himself that he had begun in those boyhood days in Cork, living under but resisting the joy-denying code that was his home's inheritance. The conscious discovery of the lyrical self made an evolution in style and a mellowing of tone inevitable.

Style and tone are eminently important measures of the writer. Where they come from is interesting; what they finally express is the whole point of the writer's work. O'Faolain has called that expression "the literary personality," defining it as "what we win from life for literature."[101] He believes that the artist's primary task is to convey a unique manner of seeing. In the late 1940s O'Faolain seems to have become acutely conscious of his artist's manner of seeing.

I do not wish to suggest that his writing is in any way complacent after *The Bell* years. In fact, he seems happier in the continuance of struggle, reassured by what he cannot know, sensing that his artist's task is to engage himself in perpetually renewing mystery. He does so in a spirit that is often comic, based on the pleasure of engagement, not at all on complacency. His pursuit of happiness was itself a rebellion against the sour sides of "Faith, Fatherland, and Family" (his words for his inheritances). His work was also becoming more profoundly rebellious in its greater individuality and in its more precise social criticism.

He was an established writer whose return to private study allowed him greater freedom to reckon the world without subjecting his vision to the needs of immediate persuasion. He recognized that "there is, ultimately, no such state of mind for a creative writer as total detachment."[102] But to be in a constant rage against his society was to doom himself, he felt, to an uncreative life, which would in turn be a surrender to the anticreative forces he opposed.

He realized that he had to accept his material—what had happened to him and to his generation—without necessarily approving of it. He became more curious and less angry about his life's obsessions, and he freed himself to speak of them more fully. Distance and detachment are to him aspects of liberaton, not escape.

He also freed himself from the burden of moral solemnity. Never a moralist in the orthodox sense, nor a reformer by temperament, O'Faolain made his fiction more personal by widening his affections, even while exposing folly. The tonal result is a unique mixture of contrary moods. I have mentioned his tendency to mix trenchant irony with humorous good will. A brief illustration is this opening passage from the story "Childybawn," published in *The Finest Stories of Sean O'Faolain*:

> When Benjy Spillane's mother got a letter signed "A True Friend" informing her that Benjy had been "Carrying on" for years with a young lady in the bank she at once sank beneath all the appropriate maternal emotions. She saw her treasure looted, her future imperilled, her love deceived. She saw her poor, foolish child beguiled, his innocence undermined, his sanity destroyed. At this time Benjy was just turned forty-one, a cheerful man-about-town with a winy face like a hallow-e'en turnip with a candle inside it, a pair of merry bull's eyes, a hint of grey at his temples, and his overcoat hung down straight from his paunch as if he was going to have a baby.[103]

Like John O'Sullivan of the earlier "The Old Master," Benjy is another of the emergent O'Faolain class of ageing bachelors, in this case also an Irish "mother's man." Benjy is not as pathetic as O'Sullivan; he has more autonomy and more potential for change. O'Sullivan is a symbolic victim in the Cork of O'Faolain's vision; Benjy is both victim and escape artist, an object of O'Faolain's ridicule and admiration. In spite of everything silly that Benjy has been made into, he *has* been "carrying on," that is, taking a hand in the creation of his life. He is a symbol of his repressed cultural environemnt; yet, by partially overcoming that repression, he is a reflection, tangentially, of O'Faolain's sentiments. In fact, all of O'Faolain's later comedies are "problem comedies" in that they balance human foible with individual virtue. Moral crisis is there, but it is less ponderous than in the earlier stories. On the other hand, there is a more subtle linkage between the writer and his material.

Though at the peak of his powers, O'Faolain found himself turning away from the novel (he burned three attempts) and toward the short story as his one fictional medium; as compensation, he occasionally wrote long tales with more complicated and loosely bound structures, and sometimes peopled his stories with sophisticated or intellectually oriented characters. Though these figures are more complex than is traditional in the Irish short story, they are put into recognizable Irish situations, thereby keeping the reader's expectatoins within the limitations of the story's crisis. The characters are not so autonomous that they act as points of departure from storytelling, yet they are a medium for thematic enrichment. An example is the characterization in "Lovers of the Lake,"[104] concerning two adulterous lovers, middle-aged, modern, and well-to-do, who spend a penitential weekend together at Lough Derg, a religious retreat island that is medieval in its harsh accomodations. This tale has been singled out by several critics for special praise, particularly for its contemporaneity. It is more open-ended, ambiguous, and suggestive of a chapter in a novel than is usually expected in a short story.

Though he was not writing novels, in 1956 he published a study of the novelists of the 1920s, *The Vanishing Hero*, an expansion of a lecture series he gave at Princeton University in 1953. During the 1930s and 1940s he had written about a dozen essays on the novel, particularly on the genre's relationship to social conditions. *The Vanishing Hero* examines the disintegration of the social concept of heroism (the hero representing a social code) in the modern novel, and it considers the ambivalent state of the genre as a result. Though several of O'Faolain's own protagonists are subversive, they reveal a need for a social life to which they can contribute. O'Faolain speaks out of a novelist's experience with difficulties also faced by the best novelists of the day, including Faulkner, Greene, Waugh, Hemingway, Joyce, and others.

The Vanishing Hero provides many insights into O'Faolain's own creative priorities. He writes a fine but qualified appreciation of Graham Greene, for example, which reveals how far apart Greene and he are. O'Faolain states:

Everything he writes is rigged to demonstrate that human nature is rigged against itself. Besides, and this above all, Greene is not in the least interested in finding interim or human solutions to any problem that he poses. He wants situations in which (symbolically) there can be no solutions of a purely human nature.[105]

These tendencies are contrary to O'Faolain's humanistic spirit, yet he is attracted to Greene's daring conceptions and his way of making the novel a serious form. One of O'Faolain's conclusions, however, is that "what he is writing is not so much novels as modern miracle plays."[106] He believes that religious thought is but one of several fictional means for evoking truth and for producing serious themes.

His comments on Greene recall his previously published study of John Henry Newman, *Newman's Way*,[107] which illustrates O'Faolain's tendency to balance the world against the spirit. He finds Newman interesting for both the trivialities of his background and for the profundity of his personality. Newman's early life and family connections are emphasized and detailed. One critic, Hilary Jenkins, has suggested that O'Faolain is defending his own propensity toward memory-life in describing Newman's passion for his past.[108] Those apparent trivialities of background are understood as important symbols of the soul's journey.

O'Faolain's writing during the 1960s is highlighted by a memory motif, and to read his work of that decade is to look at his own recollections. His characters begin to age with him, and they have pasts which they both tread upon and trip over. *The Heat of the Sun*,[109] *I Remember! I Remember!* and *Vive Moi!* (two story collections and an autobiography) deal with the power of the past to both illuminate and threaten present life. He begins the title story, "I Remember! I Remember!" with a direct but provocative statement.

I believe that in every decisive moment of our lives the spur to action comes from that part of the memory where desire lies dozing, awaiting the call to arms. We say to ourselves, "Now I have decided to do so-and-so," and straightway we remember that for years and years we have been wanting to do this very thing. There it is, already fully created . . . . [110]

35

The implications of such a statement are numerous. What has hidden this desire? What makes a decisive moment happen? How can memory preserve something unbeknownst to the rememberer? How can desire have been "created"? O'Faolain's later stories elaborate upon questions such as these. These memory questions are really personality questions, for as one reviewer of *I Remember! I Remember!* pointed out, mere recollection of fact lacks fascination, whereas recollection filtered by personality is exciting.[111]

I Remember! I Remember! includes three stories I have mentioned in connection with O'Faolain's youth, "The Sugawn Chair," "Love's Young Dream," and "A Touch of Autumn in the Air." These are remarkable stories, evocative of the seduction of old affections, yet ironically precise about the self-delusions that make those seductions possible.

In *Vive Moi!* it is clear that the themes of O'Faolain's memory-stories are the themes of his own personality. This work brings together a self-critical intellect and a celebrating spirit, balancing both instincts against each other. In spite of its title (which is simply an acknowledgement of the mystery of selfhood), there is no pomp in his theme. *Vive Moi!* is, however, an assertion of the creative and personal life (less as an exclusive gift and more as a general inheritance or birthright). On the last page of the autiobiography O'Faolain refers to memory and creativity as follows:

> If once the boy within us ceases to speak to the man who enfolds him, the shape of life is broken and there is, literally, no more to be said. I think that if my life has had any shape it is this. I have gone on listening and remembering. It is your shape, O my youth, O my country.[112]

To O'Faolain, the artist is unique in his consciousness of these relationships and in the fact that he gives them form. And rendering or discovering form is the artist's way of taking possession of his total experience, past, present, internal, external. Finally, form expresses both self and native land, for each depends on each for definition. In *Vive Moi!* he handles his youth and his country somewhat roughly but with fidelity.

Several characters in *The Heat of the Sun* also attempt to take emotional possession of their lives. The stories deal with their being made aware of their submerged but restless desires, of the possibility of fulfillment, and of the repressions that make fulfillment difficult. Often the repression is embodied in a kind of respectability. Of an ageing but lately amorous bachelor in the story "Dividends," O'Faolain writes: "It is the sort of thing that can easily happen to men who have lived all their lives by the most rigid disciplines, and then suddenly get sick of it all and throw their hats over the moon."[113] These lines also exemplify a tendency in O'Faolain's later fiction toward direct narrative voice. In fact, in "Dividends" and in other stories of the collection, the narrator is called Sean—an onlooker within the story. His characters seem his associates—an illusion he continues to create throughout his late fiction.

From the late 1950s to the late 1960s, O'Faolain did some foreign travelling and spent a few semesters at American universities as a visiting writer. He revisited the New England of his youth in 1964 (Boston College) and in 1966 (Wesleyan University). The Boston stay probably evoked the story called "The Planets of the Years,"[114] a reflection in wintry Cambridge upon geographical and temporal exile through the characters of old and young Irishwomen. Told from the young woman's perspective, the story carries a special sensitivity through her understanding of what she has in common with the old woman.

Women are often the most significant characters in *The Heat of the Sun* and the next collection, *The Talking Trees*. The range of types is in itself impressive, and, as John V. Kelleher accurately said of O'Faolain in 1957: "He likes women; he is one of the few Irish writers who really do; but he insists on regarding them as people and therefore responsible."[115] His women characters have choices and exert power, and yet he fully realizes the constraining forces that impose upon them.

Some of the interesting women in the two collections are: Lottie Black, an ageing siren of the music hall ("Billy Billee"); Janey Anne Breen, a shrewish young wife and strong arm of the Ladies' St. Vincent de Paul ("One Man, One Boat, One Girl"); Barbara Plunkett, a naive beauty who cannot understand her effect on men ("A Sweet Colleen"); Jenny Rosse, an imaginatively faithless, physically faithful wife ("A Dead Cert"); Rita Lamb, a married woman who loves a priest ("Feed My Lambs"); Daisy Bolster, the fast schoolgirl who "educates" the boys ("The Talking Trees"); Mary Anne Gogan, an ageing spinster who experiences an Italian romance ("Liars"). There is nothing sentimental or evasive about any of these portraits.

Perhaps the best female-characterization of all is in the story "The Kitchen." It is based on O'Faolain's remembrance of his own mother's old age in the house on Half Moon Street. The story of her grimly defended kitchen is a rather special self-expression for him. Like many of his stories, it is both ironic and compassionate. It pierces, as O'Faolain hoped it would, into the "darkness of memory which, in the end, only fiction can dispel."[116]

The tale arises out of the old woman's traditional fear of the encroaching landlord (he merely wishes to expand his bootmaking business into another room — her kitchen). This situation objectifies her as a type.

> . . . there is not a peasant widow woman from the mountains of west Cork to the wilds of Calabria who does not feel her kitchen as the pulse and centre of her being as a wife and mother. That red-tiled kitchen had been my mother's nest and nursery, her fireside where she prayed every morning, her chimney corner where she rested every night, the sanctum sanctorum of all her belongings, a place whose every stain and smell, spiderweb and mousehole, crooked nail and cracked cup made it the ark of the covenant that she had kept through forty years of sweat and struggle for her lost husband and her scattered children.[117]

There is power in this conception and its expression, but the story expands its significance beyond type behavior into the personal.

> She was a grand old warrior. She fought her fight to a finish. She was entirely right in everything she did. I am all for her. Still, when I switch on the bulb over my head I do it only to banish her, to evict her, to push her out of *my* kitchen, and I often lie back to sleep under its bright light lest I should again hear her whispering to me in the dark.[118]

Theme, character, and author coincide here in a special way. Memory, expressed in all its moral, fearful, yet seductive power, rises up out of characterization to the level of the writer himself.

O'Faolain's most recent books are sophisticated reflections upon ageing. *Foreign Affairs and Other Stories* concerns itself with exotic, unexpected adventures in later life. Middle-aged and beyond, the protagonists encounter the unconventional, not by chance but by an inevitable evolution of their submerged desires. They are surprised to find that those old desires have not died, that in fact they have become "foreign," almost unrecognizable for all their years of internalization. It is no longer a case of memory-theme, but of the importance of the forgotten and ignored parts of internal life. Most of the characters are people of active-life: doctor, lawyer, antique-dealer, travel-agent, dressmaker, and diplomat. But it is the hitherto inactive parts of their beings that emerge in these tales. For the man or woman of the world, there is still — even in age — a possibility of emotional maturation.

The foreign affairs of these stories often involve amorous adventure. Love and sexuality are O'Faolain's old themes through which he shows the ascendancy of the personal over the societal. His recently published novel, *And Again?*, is a kind of fantasy on love affairs engaged in by a man living a second life. The gods allow Robert Younger to live again, purely for experimental reasons. What they offer him is a new life in reverse, beginning at age sixty-five and progressing towards a second youth, childhood, infancy, and ultimate nothingness. He loves three women as they grow older and he younger: a mother, daughter, and granddaughter. The novel is partially a celebration of the mythic search by man for woman, a search not just for love but for a unity of all the lives of man — his seven ages. Younger's greatest love, O'Faolain's image of the feminine ideal, is Nana, the graddaughter, who provides Younger with all manners of affection and understanding that his many ages require. She is capable of accepting the miracle of his rebirth and becomes his confidante, lover, wife, and ultimately, as he shrinks into second childhood and infancy, mother. She is as fascinated as he is with his miraculous life. She helps him to unite his end with his beginning, sharing his memories of his second life, his research into his former life, and by means of love helping him to intimate the primary affections of that first life.

And so old age, youth, and their memory-links are the subjects of O'Faolain's old age. He sees his own life and the life of man as multiple and integral at once. It is fitting that his *Collected Stories*[119] have recently been published in large volumes on both sides of the Atlantic, for as an entire group the stories give a picture of the artist's whole life. Six new tales appear at the end of the collection. Like *And Again?* they are full of literary allusion, including touches concerning or mindful of Stendhal, Browning, Yeats, George Moore, and Henry James. These suggest a late-life interior dialogue with writers who have mattered to O'Faolain, a dialogue that also suggests why writers do matter.

He and Eileen live south of Dublin in Dun laoire, not far from James Joyce's martello tower at Sandycove. (It is in this fitting locale that Robert Younger begins his second life.) In a private, quiet way O'Faolain continues to write, read, and lend encouragement to young writers. His daughter Julia is now a widely respected fiction writer. She has described his youthful old age in an article entitled "Sean at Eighty."[120] To meet him is to be surprised by a light step and humorous eyes, and by an indifference to the sentimentalities of the past. For a writer who has made so much of what has been, his true subject remains the now that the past creates.

CHAPTER TWO

Nationality and Beyond

Patriotic, cultural, and social Ireland are O'Faolain's thematic resources, both as creative writer and social critic. That he and his literary contemporaries should concern themselves with the matter of Ireland is not surprising, given the inheritances of a literary renaissance and a political revolution. O'Faolain's generation of Irish writers began its work around 1930, overlapping by a few years the later careers of several Literary Renaissance figures. Augusta Gregory died in 1932, George Moore in 1933, AE in 1935, Yeats in 1939. And, though so vigorously separate in life, Joyce seemed to have joined that elder generaton by his death in 1941. O'Faolain met his literary elders when they were ageing legends; he and his contemporaries were imbued with their aura, and came to know their art intimately.

Those earlier writers were mostly Anglo-Irish Protestants, rooted in the established ruling class. Those who were born Catholic, like Moore and Joyce, had closer ties to the aristocracy than to the peasantry. Though most of these writers were not wealthy (Joyce's poverty is rather famous), they were for the most part far better off economically and culturally than were the writers of the next generation. These, like O'Flaherty, O'Faolain, and O'Connor, were predominantly of native Catholic stock, with direct (e.g., O'Flaherty) or indirect (e.g., O'Faolain and O'Connor) links to the peasantry. The three representatives I name here all began their lives in economically difficult conditions.

Another telling difference between the two generations was their relationship to or involvement with the revolutionary experience. Though as a group the Anglo-Irish were ultimately the biggest losers in that period ending in the late 1920's, the younger native writers were more personally scarred by the Anglo-Irish and Civil Wars, since they came to their maturity at the time of those conflicts. The three I have mentioned were all directly involved in actual warfare.

The younger writers expressed themselves differently, mostly in realistic prose fiction rather than in verse or poetic drama. Yet, from the first their art was distinctive for its poetic quality, for they were conscious inheritors of an Anglo-Irish literary tradition.

Part of the reason for this Anglo-Irish influence is personal. At a time when the country was turning away from the social and political influence of the Anglo-Irish, Anglo-Irish writers such as Lady Gregory, Yeats, and AE were befriending and assisting young native writers. One interesting example of this conquest by kindness is the case of young Frank O'Connor. Before he met Yeats and AE he was somewhat antagonistic to them and their reputations as great Irishmen. Later, after experiencing their hospitality and profiting by their generous receptions of his work, he took them to himself as spiritual fathers, as his written tributes attest. Ultimately he venerated them. O'Faolain was quick to understand and appreciate what the earlier generation had achieved. He was particularly fond of AE, and while in America wrote to him as to a mentor. He had greater intellectual admiration for the creative personalities of Yeats and Joyce. To O'Faolain these men were models of self-realization whose lives as artists were conquests over the constraints of circumstance.

To suggest that the literary basis of this generational influence was poetic is not to imply 'poetic' in linguistic terms, though many commentators have placed most emphasis on language in assessing the development of Irish literature in English. The creative ideas of the Literary Renaissance, the ideas bequeathed to O'Faolain's generation, were themselves poetical, and lent themselves to poetic expression. In the original form, these ideas were really ideals. There was, for example, the idea or ideal of ancient Ireland's uniqueness—the espousal of an old cultural heritage. There was the associated belief in a visionary future in which a peculiarly Irish way of life could once again flourish, free of alien interference, though not necessarily of Anglo-Irish influence from within. These thoughts engendered a mythological, Kathleen-ni-Houlihan symbology, though they also carried enormous practical potential with them.

In the early Renaissance, these ideas were expressed in heroic form, as in much of the work of AE and the early Yeats. Gradually they were subjected to ironic scrutiny and even parody, as in the Irish work of George Moore, in the middle career of Yeats, and in much of Joyce. Yet these ironical treatments were not indifferent dismissals of Irish idealism; in their questioning way they were spiritual extensions of that idealism. In a 1934 essay entitled "The Emancipation of Irish Writers," O'Faolain remarks: "Irish literature, as I feel it, has always been seeking escapes from the shattering of its ideals."[1] This statement touches upon inherited idealism, realization of its failures, and yet the young Irish writer's desire to be saved frm the loss of idealism itself. The statement speaks of the literary inheritance of his own generation, one that can be called a lover's quarrel with Irish idealism.

Considering that the Literary Renaissance had so concerned itself with Irish nationality in an era of national revival, and that O'Faolain's generation witnessed the ultimate crisis of that revival, it was inevitable that the younger writers would continue to assess what it meant to be Irish and to consider the practical results of the previous generation's cultural ideals. O'Faolain and his contemporaries also had to deal with the evolution of popular, political versions of those ideals, which were often quite opposed in spirit to the creative impulse that had given them origin.

He became the most vigorous cultural spokesman of his generation of Irish writers, particularly during the early 1940s when as editor of *The Bell* he opposed the latter-day Irish Ireland doctrines of the DeValera establishment. Irish Ireland mentality had developed out of the Sinn Fein movement and the Gaelic League's aim to reestablish the Irish language as the cultural basis of the new Ireland. Early Irish Ireland thinking had been congenial to most of the writers of the Literary Renaissance, who, though writing in English, thematically associated themselves with Gaelic revivalism. In the postrevolutionary period, however, many of the more extreme nationalists took these cultural aims and radicalized them into blunt prescriptions for a Catholic and Gaelic state, purified of non-Catholic, non-native influence.[2] To O'Faolain, Irish Ireland became a falsifcation of the creative impulse that had nourished the early Gaelic League, the Literary Renaissance, and his own youthful Gaelicisation in West Cork; for Irish Ireland was not as concerned with Irish uniqueness as it pretended to be; it was concerned with asserting a mythic Irish superiority, simply by turning away from the rest of the world. He saw this kind of thinking as deliberate obscurantism and deluded partiotism, a sublimation of an old Irish inferiority complex toward Europe, and a threat to a progressive future for his countrymen.

O'Faolain's opposition to what was at the time the prevailing ethos can be seen as a continuation of an intellectual individualism formerly espoused by the Anglo-Irish intellectual minority. It is clear, for example, that Horace Plunkett's and AE's *Irish Statesman*, which between 1919 and 1930 had been a voice of vigorous social criticism, was a spiritual ancestor of *The Bell*, begun by O'Faolain in 1940. Involved with national passions since its beginning, modern Irish literature had often thrown up the adversary voice, from both nationalistic and pluralistic points of view. In prerevolutionary days, idealistic nationalism had itself been a minority movement, and as such had special appeal to literary men like Douglas Hyde, W.B. Yeats, and John M. Synge. Hyde's "de-Anglicization," Yeats's mystic nationalism, and Synge's vision of the peasantry were aspects of a cultural revolution against external domination.

Ultimately, however, Irish writers (often the same cultural revolutionaries) opposed the more narrow-minded aspects of the nationalist movement. Douglas Hyde, founding president of the Gaelic League, fought a losing battle against Irish Republican Brotherhood influences within his organizaton. By 1915 the League had become so politicised and anti-intellectual in its motives that Hyde resigned his twenty-one year presidency. The early history of the Abbey Theatre is often a story of conflict between aesthetic and propagandistic intention. The very relationship between dramatist and audience in Yeats's heyday was challenging and sometimes belligerent. The Dublin audience did not trust its playwrights, particularly because it saw them as members or allies of the Protestant Ascendancy.[3] And because that audience had little intellectual or literary sophistication, it often mistook intellectual honesty and aesthetic purpose for expressions of anti-Irish feeling. The *Playboy* riots of 1907 were the most blatant expression of that mistrust. Because of who he was, Synge, descended from the Protestant ruling class, could not treat his peasant characters with affectionate humor, nor admire them in unorthodox ways, without being hated as a calumniator of Irish national virtue. From the days of Synge on through the postrevolutionary era, sentimental nationalism emerged as the basis for most attacks on artists and works of art. Writers counterattacked with increasing frequency, particularly after the widespread banning of books by the Censorship Board, which began its work in 1930. O'Faolain was a vigorous condemner of what had effectively become anti-intellectual nationalism. He considered the censorship mentality a betrayal of revolutionary aims and a sign of "nationalism-in decay."

For O'Faolain and his artistic contemporaries, then, raised at the tail end of the colonial era, fired by the events of 1916, tried by actual involvement in revolution and civil war, and alienated by a period of cultural atrophy in postrevolutionary times, patriotic inheritance cut in two opposite directions. They were inheritors of a powerful patriotic imagery, from Cuchulain to Kathleen-ni-Houlihan, from Thatched Cottage to Western Isle, and from Blood Sacrifice to Gunman's Shadow. These kinds of images sustained them for a time, but when they began to seek new life beyond the images, they experienced hostility and found that they had also inherited the artist's alienation from the popular patriotism, though they had shared in that patriotism's creation and growth.

These conflicting and trying inheritances led some writers to choose exile; other responded by engaging in intellectual missionary work at home. After his American interlude, O'Faolain took the latter course, attempting to exorcise the Irish mind of dead-end provincialism and patriotic fundamentalism. Besides his *Bell* editorials and his articles in other journals, the main sources of his Irish commentary are his biographies, particularly those on Constance Markievicz (1934), Daniel O'Connell (1938), Eamon DeValera (1939), and Hugh O'Neill (1942)[4]; his first three novels, a *A Nest of Simple Folk* (1934), *Bird Alone* (1936), and *Come Back to Erin* (1940); his travel book on Ireland, *An Irish Journey* (1940); his short history, *The Story of Ireland* (1943)[5]; and his cultural history, *The Irish* (1947).

This list rightly suggests that he was most active as a social and cultural commentator during the 1930s and 1940s. Yet, he continued thereafter writing journal articles on Irish manners and developing a subdued social analysis in his later fiction. Commenting on his later stories, Patricia Craig aptly notes their concern with "the condition of Irishness" rather than "the condition of Ireland."[6] In that later body of work O'Faolain speaks less of the problems of Irish history and more of that history's effects on the living Irish. One effective way he does this is by means of his characters' memories. Confronting new and even alien experience, they remember themselves as Irishmen and Irishwomen, people of old Irish places and habits. "Two of a Kind," a story about two Irish exiles (collected in *I Remember! I Remember!*), and "Dividends," about late-life romance (in *The Heat of the Sun*), are particular examples of this much-used memory motif.

O'Faolain's literary personality is the true basis of his social and cultural vision. He sees in the artist's individualism and mental freedom a paradigm for the Irish people, who he believes are evolving toward greater imaginative and intellectual freedom. A vital part of his analysis of Irish life, therefore, is his assessment of the writer's place in it, for the condition of life the writer experiences and the quality of art he produces are a measure of the country's cultural health.

In "The Pleasures and Pains of Ireland," an editorial published in *The Bell* in 1944, O'Faolain writes of the first of these measures (condition of life), suggesting that the Irish were still experiencing an "unfinished revolutionary period"; a formal society with a perfected art of living was still beyond them. He speaks of an Irish national mystique that had not yet filtered into formal conventions and actual techniques, such as in "laws, food, music, painting, sport, dress, architecture." In this transitional period from folk world to civilized society, the artist had to struggle in a kind of cultural limbo. Turning away from the once-nourishing imagery of the folk world, he found little ready-made subject matter, and when he chose to criticize Irish life, he was treated with intolerance, or worse, indifference. And yet O'Faolain believes that the Irish writer, if he is going to stay in Ireland, must serve his own people ("to whom we are tied by so many memories") by keeping "our ideas close to the ground because our people live close to the earth," and by making his art out of what is, not what has been or what he hopes will be. In this spirit, O'Faolain hopes for more tolerance in his society.

Well . . . . Who knows? Perhaps, down there in that once
seventh city in Christendom, some day, a leader of a government may dine with a leader of an opposition, a Catholic
Archbishop sup with a Protestant Provost, even a banned
novelist with the censor who banned him. It is, one thinks,
looking out again at that dim fabric of the capital and at
the low, far horizons of three counties, such a lovely country
to look at, its Happy Men are such good companions, it has
so much natural warmth and natural wisdom: a very little
more and a very little less — shorter memories, longer rope
for everybody, less peasant caution, more courage, more effi-
ciency, more tolerance, and She would be — shall we say She
will be — the land we all dreamed of thirty golden years ago.[7]

Perhaps it was unrealistic in 1944, when Ireland was still shak-
ing off its colonial trappings, to wish for honest humility where there
had been humiliation and a counterpart in desperate pride, for
sophistication where there had been intellectual isolation, and for
tolerance where there had been sectarian and cultural exclusivism.
And yet O'Faolain took heart regarding his country's cultural potential, mainly because of the significant achievements, against opposition, of modern Irish writers.

Those achievements had their roots in the nationalist move-
ment, but they flowered in the clearer air of universal art.
O'Faolain acknowledges the patriotic impetus behind the Literary
Revival, crediting Young Ireland's movement of the mid-
nineteenth-century as the mainspring of modern Irish writing in
English. He considers poets such as Thomas Davis and James
Clarence Mangan as rebel legend-makers rather than practical
revolutionaries. Yet, he comments on Young Ireland that

they did not devote their great talents to literature for its
own sake: they devoted them to literature in the interests of
politics. Their interest was in a functional literature. Their
literary work suffered accordingly; their political influence
prospered.[8]

O'Faolain points out that Young Ireland's most vital effect on the
Literary Renaissance was in its political idealism, which he judges
too propagandistic and locally motivated for a developing
literature.[9] It was Young Ireland which nurtured the myth of the

"legendary greatness" of the Irish people, a credo to the later Irish Ireland movement. Yeats and the many writers influenced by Yeats set about to purge Irish literature of what O'Faolain calls "political impurity," doing so by emphasizing the individualistic and the universal in Irish life.

This is not to suggest that for O'Faolain and his contemporaries success as writers depended upon intellectual detachment from nationalistic passions, nor that there was no choice for them but to follow in Yeats's footsteps. As writers and Irish people they were affected by Young Ireland's emotional nationalism, as were their opponents in the Abbey audiences, on the Censorship Board, in government, in the church leadership and in the press. The Irish Theatre and Abbey plays that had incurred the most nationalist hostility, and that continued to do so in O'Faolain's time, were often passionately Irish in their motivation. Yeats's *The Countess Cathleen* (1899), Synge's *Playboy of the Western World* (1907), and O'Casey's *The Plough and the Stars* (1926) shared little except their Irishness of emotion and their espousal of individual freedom. It was this latter element that was felt to be most threatening to the collectivist passions of nationalist audiences. The common accusation made against these works was that they were slanders against the Irish people. Opponents of the plays, using the rhetoric of politics, defended a collectivist idea of Irishness against the interests of individual Irish life expressed artistically. This political attitude was not necessarily more patriotic than the artistic attitude.

This clashing of passions did not evenly divide all artists from political nationalists. A prime exception is Daniel Corkery, whose career as writer and scholar developed in a nationalist direction, even while his former followers, O'Faolain and O'Connor, were turning toward greater individualism and universalism. Though his early influence as literary mentor had been vital, Corkery's long-range influence on the two younger writers was more fruitful in his antagonism, for he became a catalyst of the cultural and moral forces in Ireland that they felt called upon to oppose. The fact that a close friend and supporter had become a literary enemy also had a maturing effect upon their visions of their country's problems. In *An Only Child* O'Connor speaks of Corkery's opting for "the imaginative improvisation of the community" over that of the artist.[10] Generous, pious, and modest, Corkery was intensely energetic as a

48

teacher and literary man. Yet, his political earnestness made him dogmatic and overbearing. O'Connor thinks of him as typical of "the provincial intellectual," a self-made thinker who ultimately had too little confidence in his artist's trade when he compared it to the exploits of patriotic heroes.[11] Corkery had in fact been friends with the two famous Cork martyrs of the times, Terence MacSwiney and Thomas MacCurtain. In a 1936 essay about Corkery published in *Dublin Magazine*, O'Faolain judges that his elder's true literary personality, gentle and intimate, had been drowned by his admiration for the masculine and belligerent.[12]

Indeed, Corkery's work displays a strange mixture of artistry and zealotry. As a writer of fiction, his artistic models were the nineteenth-century Russian realists, an influence he passed along to his young followers. He transposes the Russian touch for common life into his own handling of Irish peasants and urban poor. At his best, he bestows a Hawthornesque sense of mystery to his people and the land they inhabit. Stories like "Carrig-an-Afrinn," "The Ploughing of Leaca-na-Naomh," and "The Stones" reveal this power, each being a tragedy of Irish introspection, told with an air of superstitious morality. In each story, tragedy arises out of an offense against native pieties regarding the spirit of the land. Stories like these are telling revelations of Corkery's personality, so aware of the dangers of obsessive belief and yet so subject to it himself.

In his less successful fiction, Corkery's morality becomes more blatant and propagandistic, but its basis is the same; that is, that native tradition is holy, that modern or alien influence is evil. In these stories, he seeks, as O'Faolain says, "the historical Irish peasant fated to resurgence."[13] "The Wager," one of Corkery's best-known tales, is an exciting but bluntly nationalistic piece contrasting a decadent, flabby gentry (Anglo-Irish) with a disciplined, high-bred peasantry (native). "Nightfall" is thematically similar; it contrasts a spiritually bankrupt "Colonial" (a returned expatriate) with a passionate native stock (young people who have never left their homeland). This broad moral categorization is part of Corkery's abandonment of the delicate, sympathetic vision he had inherited from Chekhov and Turgenev; it also runs counter to the nondidactic aesthetic of the Literary Renaissance. Corkery was attempting to be bold and new, but the effect was sometimes quite opposite. O'Faolain judges this bluntly moralistic side of Corkery as a seeking after strength that is more "a confession of weakness when the search produces a conventional idealization that only impresses one with a sense of somebody blowing up a balloon."[14]

One Corkery story, "The Ruining of Dromacurrig," seems a precursor of opposite intention to O'Faolain's "Midsummer Night Madness" in its handling of the Big House in decay. Corkery describes that decay as the just inheritance of a weak and corrupt master, cursed by his wrongful authority over his peasants. O'Faolain depicts prodigality, but he does not moralize it as the cause of ruin. On the contrary, he sympathizes with old Henn's lust for life, which seems superior to the small-mindedness of the "freedom-fighter, " Stevie Long.

By the time O'Faolain and O'Connor were publishing their first books, Corkery was standing in private and public opposition to them. He did not acknowledge O'Connor's gift of a signed copy of *Guests of the Nation*.[15] That year, 1931, was the publication date of Corkery's controversial *Synge and Anglo-Irish Literature*. In a review that appeared in *The Criterion*, O'Faolain took exception to Corkery's doctrinaire criticism while praising the author's personal insights.[16] The book is an aggressive development of Corkery's earlier *The Hidden Ireland* (1925), which was an idealization of the Gaelic peasant culture of the eighteenth century. Though impoverished and abused by the Penal Laws, those people were in Corkery's view "a complete and unique civilization," still involved with the poetic culture of the old bardic world. *Synge and Anglo-Irish Literature* goes farther in asserting an exclusive destiny for Irish literature, excluding, among other things, the bulk of Anglo-Irish literature as an expression of an alien people for an alien audience. Corkery prescribes a formula for the racial mind, insisting that the truly Irish writer must identify himself with the concerns of his people in the mass, particularly with their three obsessions: religion, the land, and nationalism. Unlike O'Faolain's call for earth-bound Irish writing, Corkery's formula minimizes aesthetic intention. His argument practically suggests, as one reviewer said, "that only an Irish Catholic Nationalist can write Irish literature."[17] O'Faolain deliberately counters this prescriptive view in *The Irish* by elaborating upon six "branches" of Irish life: Peasantry, Anglo-Irish, Rebels, Priests, Writers, and Politicians.

The publications of these two studies by Corkery spanned the Censorship of Publications Act of 1929 and helped to fuel public debate between Irish Ireland and Literary Renaissance views of Irish culture. By the late 1930s, O'Faolain and O'Connor were counterattacking Corkery's dogma in literary journals such as *Dublin Magazine* and *Ireland Today*. Their main concern was that Corkery was helping to popularize a myth of Irish purity in past worship, thereby giving false credibility to the "immunization" work of the Censorship Board. Corkery went so far as to attack the young writers' literary criticism for being published abroad, for concerning itself with what he considered alien tastes, and for lacking in a deliberate Irish self-identification. O'Faolain countered by warning Irish readers against impersonal, predisposed readings of literature.[18]

Much of O'Faolain's social commentary during the 1930s and 1940s is a conscious refutation of Corkery's writings. In its realistic handling of peasant Ireland, *King of the Beggars*, the O'Connell biography, is a direct rebuttal of Corkery's *The Hidden Ireland*. *The Irish*, particularly in its chapters on the Anglo-Irish and on Irish writers, presents a fusion view of Irish culture that opposes the exclusivist outlook of *Synge and Anglo-Irish Literature*. And, in an ironical way, O'Faolain's fiction often evokes an opposing kind of hidden Ireland to Corkery's: one of cultural frustration rather than of cultural integrity. He portrays Irish people who long for more than their indigenous past can provide, who seek self-realization in moral and intellectual experimentation. Though he suggests that the "innocent" charms of Ireland and the Irish often attract the foreigner, he also shows that the native Irish are not quite so innocent, and are themselves drawn to the uniqueness of foreign places and people.

Come Back to Erin employs this motif as a major theme. In fact, the book parodies Corkery's kind of hidden Ireland in the sentimental enthusiasms of St. John Hogan, a wealthy Irish-American shoe manufacturer. One a visit to Quit Rent, a rural home of his Irish relations, St. John is overcome by a combination of drink and sentimental nationalism. He is taken by his cousin Manus, a native traditionalist, to the family cowshed where, he is told, he, St. John, was born.

> The two stood belly to belly, the bottle in St. John's fist, the lantern in Manus's.
>
> "Mr. Hogan, I have the greatest possible regard for all forms of tradition. I have studied local traditions in all their

aspects. I record local tales for the Folk Lore Institute. A man came down here from Dublin with a dictaphone to hear me record the memories of the past. Do you know that? A great invention!" he added in a voice that somehow made the invention personal to himself and to his memories.

St. John sat down on an upturned half-tub. He gave the bottle to Manus, watched the bubbles rise in it, and took it back, and drank.

"Tradition," he said, "is the thing we haven't got in America. But Ireland? Never changes. I came from this. I'm happy."

"Tradition," agreed the little fat teacher, as he leaned one hand on the wall, "is a great thing. That, of course, is why Frankie stands for the Republic! Why we all do!"

"He's a great young fellow," said St. John. "But then, all my family is great. Every one of them. And " — his fist aloft, and his eye roving blindly until it was fixed by the stare of the cow — " look at what we came out of!"

"There you have it!"

"I'm going to commune," decided St. John. "Would you oblige me by leaving me for a few moments?"

"To be sure. It's a proper thing to do."[19]

This kind of broad satire is counterpointed in the novel by the agonizings of Frankie, St. John's half-brother and the book's protagonist. A latter-day I.R.A. rebel (the novel's time is the mid-1930s), he escapes from the Irish police by going to the United States, where he has a love affair with Bee Hogan, St. John's American wife. She is in every way a challenge to his inbred Irish patriotism, which, he comes to see, has been an escape from himself as an individual. O'Faolain does not portray her as an alternate ideal but rather as a simple representative of her American condition. Unlike Frankie, she has no cause but personal health and happiness. It is this simplicity that makes her strange and attractive to Frankie.

A number of O'Faolain stories take up this "foreign affairs" theme with similar intention. "Viva La France," set in Cork, and "Liars," set in Italy, are two comic examples. In these stories, Irish characters take imaginative flight from limiting environments and roles by means of relationships with foreigners. This motif is a metaphor for O'Faolain's own experience as a man of the world returned to Ireland. His worldly pursuit of understanding and happiness helped to make him a unique Irish voice, confidently calling for a more life-giving Ireland.

Irish Ireland promoted the romantic notion of an unbroken link in Irish cultural history between modern Irish peasant life and the old Gaelic order which had been headed by a native aristocracy. As a keystone to this notion, Daniel Corkery's *The Hidden Ireland* portrays a downtrodden but culturally intact peasant civilization in eighteenth-century Ireland. In *King of the Beggars*, O'Faolain's most ambitious biography, he describes the lot of those same peasants a generation or so later as not only economically wretched but culturally fragmented. He acknowledges that the Gaelic traditions were a consolation to them, but little more. In fact, the folk poets' tendency to sentimentalize the old Gaelic aristocrasy was, he asserts, an idealization of a class that had despised the peasantry and blocked their progress as effectively as would their English lords.

O'Connell revived them, O'Faolain argues, not by directing their loyalties backward toward the Gaelic chiefs but forward toward their own political enfranchisement, a first step in an evolution toward democratic nationhood.[20] O'Connell's persistent pragmatism is more heroic to O'Faolain than the Gaelic memory.

> O'Connell is our first successful nationalist of major size precisely because, in his realism, he accepted the principle of change. He refused to be dominated by any historical mystique, he cut away the past, he adapted himself to his own times, he never allowed any idol to tyrannize over him. In the sense that O'Connell was an European we might say that while serving the Irish people day and night he refused to allow "Ireland" to tyrannize over him.[21]

O'Faolain makes this statement in an essay entitled "The Death of Nationalism," published thirteen years before *King of the Beggars*; it sheds light upon the title and theme of the biography. In O'Faolain's estimation, O'Connell gave the common Irish a practical, political sense of themselves as a nation by releasing their natural energies to better themselves by their own efforts; by doing so, he saved them from "extermination as a distinct people."[22] Yet, O'Faolain consistently asserts that O'Connell knew the inadequacies of the people he led, both their paralyzing nostalgia for their former Gaelic masters and their habitual submission to their present English lords.

A man of decidedly democratic sympathies, O'Faolain always speaks in defense of the rights of the peasantry, but usually tempers his advocacy with criticism of their weaknesses, particularly their tendency to stagnate behind a kind of innate caution. His attitude is similar to Chekhov's toward the Russian muzhik, of which O'Faolain remarks:

> He wrote of them with sympathy that never failed him: but he wrote of them without a shadow of sentimentality. "There is peasant blood in my veins," he said once, "and you cannot astonish me with peasant virtues."[23]

O'Faolain closely echoes this statement in the following segment from *Autumn in Italy*, the book in which he says most about the peasant spirit, be it Italian, Irish, or of any culture:

> We need not romanticise the Italian peasant. I cannot. I know too much about peasants, being of peasant stock myself. They are a stock whose virtues and vices are inextricably mingled. They are conservative, cunning, cautious, . . . Yet their stubbornness has something almost heroic about it. . . . Their devotion to land, to earth, to soil, to muck is at once animal and apocalyptic. It makes them partake of the quality of some natural object which one will select according to whether one is full of admiration or exasperation — a rock, a lump of clay, a river, a pig or a bull. . . They are superstitious, yet we should respect even their basest superstitions because they are never vulgar — like the polished superstitions of city folk — and they are always related to some ancient wisdom. We have learned things that they will never know. They know things that we have long forgotten and can never again recall. They are the rhythm of nature that we have in part escaped and in part perverted. They are the youth of the world, admirable, enviable, and unbearably boring.[24]

This mixture of admiration and repulsion does not emanate from a commonplace sentimentality joined to self-superiority. Close to the peasant world himself, O'Faolain is dismayed by that world's denial of a fuller life for its own. In a review of Cecil Woodham-Smith's *The Great Hunger* (1962), O'Faolain first describes the physical horrors of the nineteenth-century Irish famine, then remarks: "The most terrifying thing about those dying hordes is that hardly a word has come down to us from their parched mouths."[25] Their silence in the face of such suffering is symptomatic of the mental exhaustion that O'Connell had struggled against.

In "A Broken World," O'Faolain writes a story about the inertia of peasant habit and the crushing frustration of a leader who tried to help these land people. Set in postrevolutionary Ireland, the story brings together three train passengers: a priest, a farmer, and the narrator. They converse as they ride through a wintry land. The shrivelled priest looks out the carriage window and calls that land "lonely." What he means is that it and its people have made *him* lonely, for he is a former parish pastor who failed in his efforts to agitate the people into a social initiative. Their age-old habit of subservience was unshakable, even after their English landlords had left. He likens their community to a body without a head, lacking "moral unity." It becomes clear after the old priest disembarks that he is known as a "character" in the region, a foolish man who, the farmer informs the narrator, had been "silenced" for his "politics." The fascinated narrator tries to pry more information out of the peasant but only scratches at his confused indifference.

"What kind of ideas had he? I mean, what did he want?"
"Begobs, I dunno."
Then he added, as if it was a matter of no importance: "He wanted the people to have the land."
"What land?"
"The land. The gentry's land."
I leaned to him eagerly—"But isn't that what ye want? Isn't that what the whole trouble is? Isn't that what the government wants?"
"Aye. I suppose it is, you know? But he wanted it to be a sudden business."
"They didn't silence him for that?"
"Maybe they didn't. Ach, he's odd. Sure, he took ten or twenty foolish young lads and, one night, he thrun down the walls of the Lord Milltown's estate. He started some sort of a league, too. He's odd. God help him."[25]

The peasant in the train is a symbol of the old priest's social analysis: a kind of headless body, a habitually lethargic being. Though they humor him with a show of respect, his peasants do not understand this rebel priest, nor do they understand or even hope for a better life.

The situation and characters in "A Broken World" resemble those in George Moore's *The Untilled Field* (1903), though Moore's purpose in handling the Irish peasant is more satiric. In O'Faolain's story, the narrator's frustration with the farmer's indifference reflects the author's more active concern about peasant problems. When the farmer drifts into sleep in his carriage seat, the narrator feels an urge "to get up and kick him."

Most of the writers of the Literary Renaissance turned their eyes toward the rural Irish world with more affection than reforming fervor; they seized upon its uniqueness in a lyrical manner, though they recorded its hardships faithfully. Yeats's and Synge's peasants had hard, unenviable lives. Nevertheless, the Abbey audience craved quaintness and nobility in peasant portrayal, and in twenty years' time exerted enough influence on the actors and writers to bring about a degeneration of the lyrical vision into a mere formula: "P.Q." — Peasant Quality, as theatre people began to call it, a sellable commodity on the Dublin stage. O'Faolain's writings about the Irish peasant administer a provocative kick, not at the peasant himself but at his idealizers. He ultimately accuses them of indifference by sentimentality, allying himself with a new breed of peasant-born writers like Liam O'Flaherty and Patrick Kavanagh.

Those who sentimentalized the peasant world tended to be offended, or pretended to be offended, by its actuality. An example was the banning of Eric Cross's book, *The Tailor and Ansty*, in 1943, when the Censorship Board and the Irish Senate considered the racy talk of an actual peasant, tailor Tim Buckley, too indecent for the public ear. The noble peasant myth was also of propagandistic value to the policy of cultural exclusivism, the pretense being that self-sufficiency and moral superiority in the common Irish peasant were proof of the same virtues in the general Irish culture, and that these virtues were strongest in the most insulated segment of the population.

Besides arguing with this propagandistic utilization of the Irish peasant, O'Faolain consistently challenged the status of the peasant as the most common or representative Irishman. In a 1943 *Bell* editorial, he speaks of a new Ireland neglected by its writers for the old.

> . . . look no farther than our novels and plays. It is a remarkable thing that they are now, virtually without exception, pictures of rural or provincial life. Yet, here is an array of new material in this new capital asking to be recorded—the emerging society of a native government, a *corps diplomatique*, a Church of unbounded influence and occasional panoply, a growing middle-class full of energy, a raw, new industrialism, a decaying gentry and an *ancien regime* that hums with echoes. . . .[27]

O'Faolain does not suggest that the short story shares in this neglect, for, in fact, these classes and types are the subjects of most of his own stories, particularly of the latter half of his career. His tales provide an intimate view of professional and urban Ireland, while Frank O'Connor's later stories develop the subject of the urban, middle-class, Irish family. Together these writers established an Irish literary trend away from the countryman toward the townsman. Their primary motivation stemmed from their townsman background; yet, at the same time that their art was maturing they both felt compelled to reject a tired and complacent peasant mythology and aesthetic.

Even when O'Faolain writes stories of rural Ireland, it is usually through the perspective of a townsman, in memory, as in "A Touch of Autumn in the Air," or in visitation, as in "The Silence of the Valley." Though "of peasant stock" himself, O'Faolain was never in fact or inclination peasant-like. He felt that his own and new Irish writing in general had a new actuality to deal with.

> But today far more than ever before there is no reason why these classes should not throw up their writers, and the peasant get a long-needed rest. If there once was an old association of the Peasant with Liberty it is all over. The romantic illusion, fostered by the Celtic Twilight, that the West of Ireland, with its red petticoats and bawneens, is for some reason more Irish than Guinness' Brewery or Dwyer's Sunbeam-Wolsey factory, has no longer any basis whatever.[28]

With this realization in mind, O'Faolain's characters range upward on the social scale from policemen, clerks, and small businessmen to teachers, artists, doctors, and public leaders.

These too are the common people as O'Faolain develops them, for their underpinning as native Irish is as humble as their achievements are significant. Behind and within them *is* a rural heritage. Their mental life ranges from the peasant to the privileged world, though they are actually somewhere between. "The Fur Coat," for example,[29] deals with an engineer's wife who cannot in good conscience own mink, though she has craved it all her adult life and can finally afford it. In her moral turmoil she blames her husband for her own reluctance, accusing him of stinginess, and, "like all the Irish," she says, of having "the peasant streak" in him. In this and other O'Faolain stories, the peasant streak is actually an inherited moral sensibility, not an aspect of moral superiority but rather a tendency toward conservatism, one which often leads to moral consternation in the face of new experience.

The common and uncommon people of Irish history are intertwined in O'Faolain's mind. Like most Irish thinkers, he believes in the messianic potential of great leadership when applied to the Irish situation, an evolution of an old people into a new nationhood. His biographies are mostly studies of great Irish leaders, and are mainly concerned with how one person has had emotional and practical impact on the evolving national mind.

As I have stated, the boy John Whelan reacted to the news of the 1916 Rising as his father did, feeling indignation with the revolutionaries; yet within a few days he was secretly praying for them and weeping over their martyrdom. This emotional revolution within him changed the direction of his life, bringing him into the rising flood of idealistic nationalism. Ten years later, when that torrent slackened, O'Faolain found himself high and dry, without a clear understanding of what had happened to his country and himself.

His biography of Constance Markievicz, published in 1934, was one of his early objectifications of that emotional experience, for in the book he judges many of the leaders of the nationalist movement before, during, and after the Rising. Of all the portraits, the most significant — aside from that of Constance Markievicz herself — are two set in contrast: those of Padraic Pearse and James Connolly, fellow Easter-martyrs.

Pearse, he points out, created no "political philosophy but . . . a heroic attitude,"[30] based on his exalted reiterations of "ancient wrongs," "ancient glories" — "a vision that by his death . . . became for ever after as sacred to all Ireland, and still remains as sacred to many as the treasure of David's ark."[31]

O'Faolain reserves greater admiration for Connolly, however. Seeing him as a hard-headed socialist republican, O'Faolain yet considers him "an idealist if to persevere in a cause too realist for one's contemporaries is idealism."[32] He singles Connolly out as the "only man of all those revolutionaries who had a shred of social policy,"[33] implying the practical shortcomings of the revolution as a long-range movement. He shares AE's feeling that Connolly was tragically lost to the country by being absorbed into emotionalist revolutionary action, and he quotes AE's statement that he "regretted his [Connolly's] Nationalist obsession because by his death Ireland lost the only labour leader it had with brains and high character."[34] O'Faolain does not reject emotional nationalism, but understands a number of its limitations. He views Connolly the man as an idealist, but one who was life-based rather than dream-based, as he himself wished to be. It is this life-based idealism that O'Faolain admires in Daniel O'Connell's personality, though O'Connell and Connolly were far apart as social thinkers. He sees these men as models of forward-looking practicality in a society given to the opposite.

Though O'Faolain judges the great by the fruits of their efforts, he also recognizes, as a man of feeling, that "Men should be measured as men, not as part of social trends."[35] On an emotional level, he is particularly attracted to revolutionary leaders who experienced alienation from the people they tried to serve. These "rebels by vocation," like Wolfe Tone, Roger Casement, and Erskine Childers, excite him as total rebels, "abberants and solitaries."[36] They embody a union of the intellectual and rebel spirit, for they possess a reckless broad-mindedness that people in the mass fear. To thinking people who observe them they are inspiring even in failure, for they leave emotional challenges to posterity.

O'Faolain asserts that these practical revolutionaries and romantic nonconformists have both worked their way, by degrees, into the personality of the Irish people. He places O'Connell, the political opportunist, and Wolfe Tone, the Young Ireland radical, at the head of each tradition. In *The Story of Ireland* he observes that

> One has only to be in the company of a group of Irishmen, on a propitious occasion, for even an hour, to become aware of the persistence of the Young Ireland spirit on the emotional plane, and of the O'Connell tradition on the intellectual plane down to our own day.[37]

Part of his optimism about human nature is his belief that exceptional people can bestow personality upon a people, based on the fact that it has happened in Ireland.

Though sectarian antagonism has been a fact of Irish life for centuries, and though the dominant mythology of modern Irish politics has made the terms nationalism and Catholicism almost interchangeable, many of the great leaders of Irish revolutionary thought have been nonsectarian in outlook. Three of O'Faolain's heroes, Wolfe Tone, Daniel O'Connell, and James Connolly, were men who tried to overcome sectarian bias in Irish life. Tone's United Irishmen sought a nationalistic alliance between Protestants and Catholics; O'Connell fought for Catholic emancipation as part of sectarian equality, not superiority; Connolly envisioned a labor movement that would cut across religious divisions, uniting all of the working class. In this regard, these men were all minority thinkers, struggling against a historical inheritance of religious intolerance, distrust, and hatred from both Protestant and Catholic sides.

This inheritance has its roots in a bitter history of actual treachery and cruelty, yet a good deal of religious separatism in postrevolutionary Ireland has also been a matter of habitual convenience. Backward-looking and uncreative, the politics of sectarianism have usually been the easiest and least challenging politics. As a Catholic with a nonsectarian social outlook, O'Faolain concerns himself most often with the evils of sectarianism from the Catholic side. In an article on Wolfe Tone published in 1946, he criticizes the moral lock-step of Catholic nationalists who allowed religious bias to bully them into dishonoring one of the nations's heroes.

60

The nation (whatever or whomever that may signify) has not yet had the courage to give him his statue. Money was collected in 1898 and it still lies in the Bank. A plaque was set in the ground at the corner of Stephen's Green to mark the site of his memorial—but the Board of Works took it up (after dark) . . . . He puts the politicians in a sad stew. They love him (secretly), commemorate him (openly) but, alas, he was a *Protestant!* He was a *suicide!* He made one or two disrespectful references to convents, bishops (who, at the time, thoroughly deserved a great many disrespectful remarks) and Catholic services.[38]

O'Faolain sees this unofficial and yet widespread disapproval of Tone the man as moral evasion in the guise of moral purity or superiority. He also feels that this kind of moral evasion has been most harmful to Catholics themselves.

O'Faolain's argument with Irish Catholicism is not over a moral crisis of faith but over morality as applied to social life. Inevitably, he has drawn closest to his religion during periods spent in Italy and the United States, where the church has been less aggressive in social matters. In Ireland, however, he often finds himself opposing Catholic conservatism's narrowing effect on Irish political, interpersonal, and individual lifestyle. Though this conflict is a major one in modern Irish literature, it may be that O'Faolain is its most outspoken and thorough analyst.

He is especially interested in mental poverty that results from moral evasion, an unrealistic response to life that he recalls as part of his upbringing.

There is one thing I do blame, because it caused me so much suffering as a boy—the delicate-mindedness, or over-protectiveness, or mealy-mouthedness, whichever it was, of the Irish Church, and the sentimentalized picture of life, especially in relation to sex, that it presented to us through its teaching orders and from the pulpit, except when some tough Redemptorist took over to give us a bit of straightfoward, realistic hell.[39]

The threat of punishment for sins bothers him less than the mental denial of physical life, the threat to make actual life less available to him as a physical and intellectual being. He sees this problem lurking behind the censorship mentality in Ireland, which he once called an attempt "to keep the national mind in a state of perpetual adolescence."[40] In a late autobiographical essay, he recalls the "mesmeric power" of his religion to make the physical world seem a deception, to liquify common life, to vaporize "the mortal into the mystical, . . . always at the expense of failing to develop the character of men as social animals."[41]

This moral timidity which leads to social backwardness is a major subject in his fiction, one which he handles in tragical, satirical, and comical modes. "The Small Lady" and "The Man Who Invented Sin" are examples of the tragic mode, for in both stories young Catholics encounter a new, broader life, yet retreat from it into their protective shells of moral "purity." In "The Small Lady," Denis, a young revolutionary in the Anglo-Irish conflict, has a sexual affair with Bela, an aristocratic captive who is being hidden (the symbolism is rather extreme) in the Trappist monastery of Mount Melleray. Realizing that her life is nearing its end, she seduces Denis, seeing in him her last chance for love in a life enjoyed recklessly. To him, she is a visitant from a strange, luxurious world of fleshly delight and mental sophistication. That world has always been beyond his reach, and he begins to explore it with Bela, passionately and imaginatively, But when his passion is spent, he also relinquishes his searching imagination, recoiling in horror at his sin, and mentally banishing Bela, her world, and the call of his own essential personality. Finally, he wishes for nothing more than a childish comfort in moral reinstatement after making his confession.

> He must keep good always now. Always and always, for ever and ever, without a single lapse. It would take a long time to forget that night in the monastery but he must not think of it again, and he was glad the priest had forbade him to go back over it. He must just take it for a lesson. He must remember that life was a hard struggle but with the help of God he would spend the remainder of it as pure as he was at that moment.[42]

It seems the ultimate in moral evasion that he should be so single-mindedly concerned with the purity of his soul while the woman he has just made love to is going to her execution.

His attitude is not much different from the resolutions of middle-aged Brother Majellan of "The Man Who Invented Sin." He is disturbed by a twenty-three-year-old memory of a cheerful holiday when, in the company of other young religious, he became friends with a young nun. Though the relationship was innocent, it reminded him of the renounced world of physical and mental freedom. Years later, he can only deal with his reverie by rejecting it, telling an old acquaintance that he disapproves of young people going on such holidays, and pronouncing that "it's not good to take people out of their rut."[43]

O'Faolain handles this kind of moral shrinkage best in satire and comedy, achieving a creative detachment from what is for him an almost obsessive theme. Though *Bird Alone* is a dark and tragic novel that turns upon the theme of moral repression and censure, it leaps to greatest life in its satiric and comic passages. For example, broad slashes of witty characterization help to establish conflict in the novel, while giving a unique Irish coloring to the moral environment. In this vein, the protagonist's pietistic father is called "Christ-on-the-Cross Crone" by his workmen, "innocent," as one of his sons says of him, "before God and disliked by every man that knew him."[44] Grandfather Philip Crone, by contrast, is a diehard Fenian in politics and is characterized by a relation as "weak in the carnalities." In one of O'Faolain' best comic scenes, Phil Crone argues vehemently with a cemetery caretaker over religious designation on a dead comrade's burial certificate. Behind the ludicrous situation is a fierce confrontation between personal integrity and moral tyrany.

> "For God's sake, now, Mr. Crone, fill in the two words—R.C.—and be done with it—the Church is wise, Mister Crone—the Church has to look after us all, dead and alive—and for God's sake and God is the best judge of all those things and God will judge you and me . . ."
>
> "What I say is, the Church wouldn't admit he was a Catholic when he was alive, so why should the Church want to say he's a Catholic because he's dead?" (I knew what he was at—the Church had banned Fenianism in Ireland.)
>
> "My dear good sir," said the man, beyond all patience, "I'm not the Church and you're not the Church, and if the Church says he was a Catholic, then it's dogma, and a Catholic he is, and no wan can get behind that. Write it down—R.C."

"The Church never admitted he was a Catholic. It denied him the sacraments. It now wants to deny him Christian burial."

The foxy man held out his index finger as if he were balancing a pin on the end of it. Solemnly he looked at it; solemnly he looked at my grander; then he tapped that finger with the tip of another, saying quietly but finally:

"Did the Church say he was a Protestant?"

"No."

He tapped his second finger. "Did the Church say he was excommunicated?"

"No!"

The man drew out a sail of a handkerchief and blew his nose. "Write down R.C.," he ordered, like a Pope.

"NO!" said my grander, and he flung down the pen in a fury. "The Church never said yiss or no to Arthur Tinsley. But you know and I know and everybody knows that no Fenian could get absolution in confession or the sacrament from the altar unless he retracted his oath to live and die for his country. And . . ."

"Mr. Crone . . ."

"And . . ."

"Excuse me, one moment, mister . . ."

"AND if Arthur Tinsley was asked here and now whether he would retract that oath . . ."

"There's nobody asking him . . ."

". . . whether, to obtain burial in this bloody cemetery, he would bow the knee to the Church, and the first question they'd put to him would be, Do you admit that oath was a sin? — what would he say? What would he say?"

The man walked away to the door.

"What would he say?" roared my grander. "He'd say: 'I wo' NOT!' And what would they say?" he bellowed, with a great sweep of his hand through the air. "They'd say: 'Then we'll have nothing to do with yeh, and yeh can go to hell'!"[45]

The scene ends with the caretaker recommending that Philip Crone appeal to the Cemetery Committee and with grandfather Crone marching out and raging: "Damn the Committee! Damn the Committee!" As a nationalist, Phil Crone is damning the Church, which had damned the Fenians. Here then is dark comedy emphasizing the vanities of both sides, through which O'Faolain generates the full vehemence of his Wolfe Tone essay, externalized into evocative social drama.

Bird Alone deals mainly with Corney Crone's sexual rebellion against the constricting morality of Catholic Cork. That rebellion is a direct descendant of the political nonconformity of Corney's Fenian grandfather. In O'Faolain's work, all moral repression is related, as are all forms of liberation. Yet, he does not suggest that it is a simple and easy matter to rebel against the dominant morality. He recognizes that the effort is often subject to the imperfections of emotionalism, vanity, and foolhardiness. His rebels, though usually likeable, are often as foolish as the order they oppose.

There is hypocrisy on both sides in the story "Unholy Living and Half Dying," a comic allegory of moral Ireland from *The Man Who Invented Sin* collection. The tale parodies the Irish sinner in the person of Jacky Cardew, an ageing club bachelor, and the Irish saint in the person of Mrs. Canty, his "crawthumping" landlady. They are aptly named, she full of pious cant, he a real card — a fun-loving fellow. Impoverished, she lives under the roof beams (nearer to heaven) in the flat above Jacky's, and twice interrupts his late-night card games (the second on Good Friday) with desperate thumpings on his ceiling. She has attacks of indigestion which she assumes to be her death throes. Twice forced to call up doctor and priest, he begins to feel her presence as a constant *momento mori*. In a moral sense, they are both like children afraid of the dark. Ironically, Jacky himself falls ill and submits to the nursing of Mrs. Canty, who comes armed with a spray of palm and a bowl of holy water.

It is a signature of his tolerant nature that O'Faolain so often allows conservative Church forces to be triumphant in fiction that challenges its authority. Like Synge before him, he allows his antagonist to possess the stage, in O'Faolain's case the stage being Irish moral life. Yet he insists that moral leadership must be honest and true to human needs. When it fails in these respects, it should expect to be challenged. O'Faolain's practical objective is to help create a balanced and healthy moral climate in his country, one that is much more tolerant than ever before.

Significant vehicles for his depiction of tolerance and intolerance are his fictional priests, who fall into two general categories: men of good will and cold symbols of moral authority. Several of the former group are modelled on Father Tim Traynor, a friend of O'Faolain and O'Connor. Traynor was an emotional person who was unafraid of his attachments to the things of this world. In "The Silence of the Valley," O'Faolain captures his nearly pagan gusto for the peasant world of Gougane Barra; in "Feed My Lambs," he dramatizes an admission that Traynor had made that he once loved the wife of a man who had wanted to be a priest (O'Connor, who sometimes fictionalizes Traynor as Father Fogarty, treats the same situation in his tale entitled "The Frying Pan");[46] in "Falling Rocks, Narrowing Road, Cul-de-Sac, Stop," O'Faolain expands upon Traynor's comments about Irish sexual sublimation.

In this story, Traynor is portrayed as fat Father Tim Buckley (the Tailor's name in real life), an amateur Freudian who gives sexual explanations for all the compulsive behavior of his parishoners.

> No wonder he was the favorite confessor of all the nubile girls in town, not (or not only) because they thought him handsome but because he was always happy to give them the most disturbing explanations for their simplest misdemeanors.[47]

His proclamation about two bachelor friends, Morgan Myles, a young librarian, and Francis Breen, an ageing doctor, is that "They have invented one another." explaining that

> "The older man needs approval for his lifelong celibacy. The younger man needs encouragement to sustain his own . . . . In fact neither of them really believes in celibacy at all."[48]

As a celibate himself, the priest knows a good deal about "sex-in-the-head," but, as O'Faolain's narrator insists, "sweet damn all about love-in-the-bed." Nevertheless, he is something of a local hero for his daring outspokenness, and when concerned friends warn him to beware of complaints to the bishop, Buckley is undaunted.

> "And," he roared, "if I can't say what I think how the hell am I going to live? Am I free or am I not free? Am I to lie down in the dust and be gagged and handcuffed like a slave? Do ye want me to spend my whole life watching out for traffic signs? Falling Rocks! Narrowing Road! Cul-de-sac! Stop! My God, are ye men or are ye mice?"[49]

O'Faolain universalizes the problem of moral stricture by having a priest complain of it. Father Tim's tirade also unites ideas of free speech with sexual and intellectual freedom. Serious social challenges are hidden in this comic tale, and, though the narrative tone is witty and apparently carefree, the problems exposed are significant. His friends laughingly answer the priest by roaring "Mice!" back at him, but he bluntly answers the flippant question of whether he intends to start a revolution by saying, "We could do worse." The "we" is, of course, the whole society, which Father Tim knows is not as content as it often pretends to be.

Though he protrays him as an emotionalist and an agitator, O'Faolain would consider Father Tim to be a highly civilized man. The civilized man is able to overcome sectarian, class and national bias, is aware and appreciative of life modes that are not his own, and understands that the life of the body is inseparable from the life of the spirit. His experience may be provincial but his values are universal, for he is willing to remake himself whenever and wherever he comes upon new knowledge.

In an editorial on the Gaelic League O'Faolain remarks: ". . . ultimately every problem is not a problem of nationality but of civilization."[50] National uniqueness is vital to a people but is not the only end of culture; an intelligent and humane technique for living must also develop. This technique is learned; the process of learning is assisted by a knowledge of the experiences of other peoples. Yet, there must first be a constructive mentality that overcomes exclusivist tendencies *within* a people.

In *An Autumn in Italy*, O'Faolain recalls an experience that imaged this potential for oneness in a people. Travelling by bus with a group of young men and women who had been to a Sicilian wine fair, O'Faolain listened to their singing almost indifferently. It was raining. Then, as he recalls,

> a cheer from the merry bus load shook me back to where I was. We had been slowed by a religious procession on the outskirts of some village. Below us on the road, in the rain, a long line of other boys and girls moved by, carrying banners and lanterns, singing hymns. My rowdy young compa-

67

nions leaned from the windows of the bus and waved their
bottles, and the boys and girls below waved and smiled
back, without halting their singing, and so we slowly passed
one another, songs and hymns mingling in the misty night.
To you, dear reader, these words can convey nothing of the
supreme pleasure that moment gave me. Life is one, is one,
I thought again and again.[51]

It was the young people's instinct for various life that so pleased him.
Pilgrims and revellers felt no antagonism toward each other and
were beyond the need for tolerance. Indeed, they identified with
each other.

The strong and protracted intolerances within Irish society are
to O'Faolain impediments to the full realization of Irish cultural life,
which should, he thinks, profit rather than eternally suffer for its
various heritage. This is his message in *The Irish*, a book which expresses the "fusion" idea of Irish cultural evolution: that all Irish
elements, including native and Anglo-Irish, Catholic and Protestant, contribute toward a common destiny. *The Irish* owes
something to AE's influence, particularly to his editorials in *The
Irish Statesman* (1923-30), which called for a synthesis between
Gaelic and Anglo-Ireland. In his book, *The National Being* (1916),
AE speaks of nation-making as only temporarily achievable by
means of conflict with an outside power. Ultimately there must be
"a fusion of diverse elements in a nation by a heat engendered from
within."[52]

AE and O'Faolain both believed that the intellectual fire of
Ireland's writers could provide that heat. Yet, if the writers were to
create a healing unity, they above all others had to understand their
country's various life modes. As young writers, O'Faolain and
O'Connor troubled themselves over their own restricted cultural experience, realizing, for example, that

> Yeats could go from Coole Park into any cabin around Gort:
> but we could not have gone from the cabin into Coole Park.
> There is the division between Yeats's generation and ours.[53]

O'Faolain, whose statement this is, is not as concerned about the
lack of privilege as about its resulting loss of sympathetic awareness
in himself and other Irish writers.

Travelling to foreign countries helped O'Faolain to overcome his social inexperience. With his own exile just ended in 1934, he recommended a similar experience to others in an essay entitled "The Emancipation of Irish Writers."

> If I had my way I should send every Irish writer of this generation out of Ireland for at least ten years, confident that he could do his best work for Ireland in the misery of exile. . . . In exile, if we could only avoid sentimentality, we might infuse into our work something of that warmth and geniality, that equanimity, good humour and love which get frozen and killed in the partisan atmosphere of home. We might even, above all, add to our literature the one thing in which it is not rich — namely, a quality of wider intellectual curiosity.[54]

He insists that a country should allow its writers to criticize it freely, yet that they should do so in an enlightened spirit, serving the country's mental health.

Such an attitude often brought O'Faolain into conflict with traditionalists, pietists, and Irish Ireland exclusivists. That his good intentions should often be misunderstood was inevitable, given "the partisan atmosphere of home." In his *Bell* editorials regarding the Gaelic League, he takes pains to explain his feelings. In one, he speaks of his generation's Gaeltacht experiences during the heyday of the Revival.

> We went to the Gaeltacht, and at once we felt an enlargement of mind and soul. We over-idealized it, but that was natural. We learned Gaelic. We delighted in the folk-lore of Gaelic, the hero-tales, the folkways, its popular songs. We brought them back to the towns and cities, and they became part of our racial mind. They gave us a little more of that precious sense of distinctiveness, and pride in proportion. Our daily lives were on another plane, and we could not live, think, feel, or work like western fishermen or country wives: it was not to be expected and if anybody suggested that we should we would have stared at him.[55]

During the early 1940s, when O'Faolain was editorializing what he called "The Gaelic Cult," Gaelic Leaguers and Irish Irelanders

were in fact making this suggestion, espousing a mystique of the old
Gaelic world as, O'Faolain states, "a model, or master-type—rather
like the National Socialist mythology of the Pure Aryan—to which
we must all conform."[56] And, when the Gaelic League began to
publish sneering attacks on Irish writers in English, including Yeats,
O'Faolain concluded that this once inspiring institution had "ruined
its mental stamina" on the drug of exclusivist politics and had lost its
cultural direction.[57] Acknowledging that for Irish people "Gaelic is
essential if we wish to inform ourselves,"[58] O'Faolain considers the
Gaelic cult more a kind of inbreeding, a desperate seeking for
security against a feared modern world.

He does not accept Ireland's inevitable separation from a
larger, more European way of life, nor does he believe in the exclusivist mythology as applied to past Irish history. O'Faolain's
essential Irishman is not the product of an inbred heritage. On the
contrary, he and his best creations are the products of a racial
blend. For example, in a travel piece called "Fair Dublin,"
O'Faolain considers the Irish capital "the most Irish because the
least Celtic city in the island, . . . the most trodden by countless
foreign and native feet . . . ."[59] In the same essay, he applies a corrective to the usual hostilities between native and Anglo-Irish points
of view.

> . . . the genius of Ireland is not an Anglo-Irish genius but a
> Celtic-Danish-Norwegian-Norman-Tudor-Cromwellian-
> English-Jewish-Irish genius—one, multiple and indivisible.[60]

Though Dublin can be seen as an architectural monument to
Anglo-Ireland, it is also, O'Faolain feels, "a true national capital"
because of the 1916 Rising.[61]

O'Faolain's fusionist view of the Irish creative spirit, which
values the individualist qualities of the Anglo-Irish and the
democratic upsurge of native Irishmen, is again similar to AE's,
which Ernest Boyd called aristocratic in thought and democratic in
economics.[62] As a cultural visionary, AE strove to create a wide
hospitality for creative individuals in Ireland. It was in this spirit
that he befriended many young writers, O'Faolain among them.
Though his thought was full of mystical idealism, he was also full of
practical wisdom on behalf of the common people. He was a leader
of Horace Plunkett's Irish Co-operative Movement, fostering

economic unity between small farmers in hopes that they could increase their share in the social order.

In his study of DeValera, O'Faolain gave that leader credit for representing the aspirations of the common people and for helping to democritize Irish social life in their behalf. Yet, unlike AE and the fusionists, DeValera lacked, as O'Faolain states, "an intelligent and indulgent interest in all classes of people and ideas,"[63] and in effect inhibited cultural growth. DeValera formed his first administration in 1932. In 1933, the year O'Faolain returned to Ireland from his American and English exile, AE left Ireland for England, where he would die two years later. A Gaelic enthusiast since his youth, he became estranged from what he called the "half-crazy Gaeldom" of Ireland after the Civil War.[64] In 1940, ten years after the demise of *The Irish Statesman*, O'Faolain founded *The Bell*. In an Irish time when every new establishment seemed to have a Gaelic name, O'Faolain named his journal after a nineteenth-century political journal, *Kolokol*, edited by a Russian liberal, Alexander Herzen. That journal, published in London but looking back at Russia, opposed oppressive government, censorhsip, superstition, fanaticism, and isolationism.[65] *The Bell* was therefore rightly named, though it also had a literary mission—to create an Irish readership for Irish writers. O'Faolain encouraged both his readers and his writers to appreciate the reality of the local as a part of a world-sense. The traditional Irish world is both preserved and criticized in the pages of *The Bell*. In an editorial entitled "1916-1941: Tradition and Creation," he writes:

> Tradition is like the soil that needs turning over . . . . It has to be manhandled, shaken up—and sometimes given a rest. It is not those who question ritual who kill it. They get to know it better and add to it by that knowledge, and add to it even while they rebel against it.[66]

The truth of this statement is more apparent today than when it was written, for though O'Faolain and his literary contemporaries might have seemed iconoclastic in the 1940s, their work now seems a window on a traditional Irish world that is barely apparent elsewhere. In daring to criticize that traditional world, they have revivified it as an aspect of universal cultural understanding.

71

O'Faolain has always seemed to be aware of this potential in Irish subject matter. For the writer and the man, the country has always counted for a great deal, yet it is not so much a change as a confirmation in his attitudes when he says as an old writer that "Ireland is worth my attention only when it is the world."[67]

CHAPTER THREE

The Spirit of Physical Life

In "The Talking Trees," a group of Cork boys go one night to the house of Daisy Bolster, who for a fee has promised to show her unclothed body to them. Their morally protective environment makes this event portentious for all of them, but most especially for Gong Gong, the most naive and imaginative of the gang. Yet, Gong Gong hardly looks at the girl as she stands naked before them. While the others stare in wonder at her anatomy, Gong Gong perceives her as Beauty itself; for in his dazzled imagination, Daisy's lamplit flesh dominates the night, the stars, the Mardyke tree-lane leading from her house, and his own romantic future. Gong Gong has the imaginative potential of the artist, already sensing the nearly spiritual animation of flesh and revelling in the evocative power of atmosphere. Through his main character, O'Faolain helps us to experience these same things, though with a touch of ironic detachment.

O'Faolain once told me that he could not see a person unless he could also see the person's ambience. He did not mean mere physical setting but more the effects of place and time as they make contact with a personality. He expressed his objective as an attempt to "see through," not at, or even around, the character. Character then becomes a means, or a medium, in the search for meaning.

This technique of developing atmosphere and theme as an extension of characterization evokes a feeling of correspondence in all of his fiction, a connection, from story to story, of a people and their meanings. Yet, he treats his themes more subtly as he matures, generally by narrowing the scope. For example, an early story such as "A Broken World" deals with problems that afflict the whole Irish peasantry, while a late story such as "The Kitchen" evokes the "peasant streak" in one old woman of Cork. The early "The Man Who Invented Sin" dramatizes religious authoritarianism over a generation of Irish people, while the late story, "Feed My Lambs," deals with a priest and a married woman whose affection for each other challenges their sacramental vows. Indeed, the later stories seem to grow out of the earlier like delicate hybrids out of established types.

In keeping with this change in thematic modulation (rather than change in theme), O'Faolain's style becomes less romantically elaborate and sharper in ironic resonance. This tonal and linguistic modernization is partially a reflection of the length of his writing career, and also a measure of his positive engagement with change. Nevertheless, he is always a writer of poetic zeal, a believer in the evocative power of his vision and language.

Short-story writers define their characters by placing them in crisis, reflecting a lifetime in a few decisive days, a day, or a few moments. In the modern realist tradition these moments are often overtly casual, though actually critical in some subtle way. O'Faolain typically formulates his dramatic crisis out of the coming of age (or the failure to do so) of the character's personality. I differentiate here between the character's coming of age (from youth to maturity) and his personality's full emergence from stunted or deluded existence into a more completely active selfhood. This can happen at any time in a life.

It is a romantic theme that can be treated with realistic subtlety. Coming of age in this sense is a complex matter. While arriving at a greater understanding of his life, the character detaches from some part of it (family ties, inherited beliefs, for example) while increasing his engagement with other parts (new relationships, liberating ideas). O'Faolain sees this change as an internal adventure. His characters do not usually alter their behavior, for in them coming of age is less a matter of conduct than of aspiration. If there is a moral element, it is related to the character's personal integrity rather than to social ethics. Adding to the subtlety is the fact that the moment of change often fails to hold, the dye runs, and what seemed a sign of fulfillment becomes instead a signal of a lifetime's failure to achieve potential.

Failures of personality are as much O'Faolain's subject as successes. Postrevolutionary Irish society provided him with studies in the failure of ideals, his own included, though it took him time to see those failures in a creative manner.

> As my anger gradually abated, but with my curiosity still unabated, I was, over the years after 1924, to become fascinated to understand, in sympathy, what flaws in the intricate machinery of human nature keep it from fulfilling itself wholly, from achieving complete integity other than in moments as brief, if one compares them with the whole span of human life, as a lighthouse blink.[1]

The lighthouse blink of realized personality is at the heart of many an O'Faolain story. The case of Daniel Cashen of "A Touch of Autumn in the Air" is illustrative.

A common businessman from Roscommon, neither sensitive nor intelligent, Cashen is nevertheless transfixed one day by a reverie of boyhood happiness. A coincidence of weather and imagery calls him back to a long-forgotten autumn that he spent on his Uncle Bartle's farm in the since-renamed Queen's County (now Laois). He re-experiences a sense of his own smallness under the vast sky stretching over the level bogs, vividly recalls the casual sights of a sunny day, and affectionately remembers a tumble in the fern with his cousin, Kitty Bergin. These moments represent the mythology of Cashen's submerged personality: "It was plain . . . that he was thinking of all those fragments of his boyhood as the fish-scales of some wonderful fish, never-to-be-seen . . . ."[2] And, like "a great number of busy men, who normally never think at all about the subjective side of themselves," Cashen is "overwhelmed by the mystery" of his sudden recollections when they do emerge. The story employs little more of present action than a short meeting in a hotel foyer, yet it fully reveals that this successful wool manufacturer has missed the personal, intimate part of his potential life, evidenced by the fact that he had forgotten so powerful a part of himself for almost sixty years. It is too late for Daniel Cashen to integrate his life, though when he dies he leaves his money to his country relations who still live "in what used to be called, in his boyhood, the Queen's County."

By ending the story with these words, O'Faolain evokes a sense of a lost world as well as one man's loss of youth and life, creating an air of universal mutability. When O'Faolain spoke of seeing *through* a character, he meant more than simply seeing through the little falsehoods of behavior, though that aspect is part of his task, gradually uncovering (as he says) the "hidden truth that, if one works hard enough, . . . will reveal itself when the last shred of conventional disguise falls at the story's end."[3] He means to uncover the character's naked psyche, but more important, having uncovered it, to see through that naked psyche to reality itself. It is Cashen's late-life reverie, not Cashen himself, that invites reader identification. The alluring imagery that O'Faolain renders through his character's memory is what brings the reader into the story, conjuring up a lost pastoral world that can represent anyone's lost youth or lost happiness. The ambience that extends from and surrounds Daniel Cashen is more than background to his characterization; it is the reality that most concerns O'Faolain. The rendering of Cashen's personality makes that reality more visible and dramatic.

This departure from characterization for its own sake is an essential in O'Faolain's writing. Cashen's representative value as a kind of ageing Everyman counts more to O'Faolain than his individualization. In all of his characterizations he strives to produce an identification with character-in-representative-situation, not with character alone. The coming of age theme is an O'Faolain signature that unifies his characterizations, reminding the comparing reader that character-making, as interesting and various as it is in O'Faolain, is not an end in itself but rather a medium for thematic departure.

Though he specializes in internalized characterization, an aspect of his writing that encourages identification, O'Faolain is particularly distinctive in the way he distances the reader from the character. That distancing does not obliterate identification but cuts it short, resulting in what he calls "intermittent identification" — a balance between emotional involvement and intellectual detachment. His main distancing device is irony, the hallmark of his character-making. For example, he perceives Gong Gong and Daniel Cashen as complicated emotional beings, yet he shapes them ironically as social types—the sexually naive adolescent and the personally underdeveloped businessman. While he fascinates us with their flights of imagination, he counterpoints this attraction with what he calls a sense of fate, "less interesting, less subtle but, . . . a good coagulant: i.e., the thing which is essential in every story to prevent emotional haemophilia."[4] Our urge to identify with their rich imaginative experiences is modified by our realization of Gong Gong's and Daniel Cashen's vulnerable naivete, and our understanding that they must pay for it. To the degree that they cannot see what we see of their fates, we are made separate and superior to them.

Some O'Faolain characters rise above the norm, understand themselves and their situations clearly, and in some way conquer both. They are usually a mixture of commonplace and eccentric personality, with the latter emerging in the story's crisis. The pattern of their development is not so much toward individualization, however, as toward symbolic heroism, for in becoming themselves fully they embody O'Faolain's most aggressive beliefs. The little victories of his characters are his way of expressing his optimism about the connection between intellectual courage and happiness. Their daring does not always make them happy, but it always makes happiness seem more possible for all of us.

O'Faolain's novelistic protagonists tend to fall into this clear-minded and courageous category. They suffer public defeats but win private victories. Leo Foxe Donnel of *A Nest of Simple Folk* rises above his inherited identity by means of revolutionary activity, though the condition of his life is often wretched. Corney Crone of *Bird Alone* becomes a tragic victim of his city's moral oppression, yet becomes something like a prophet of the place, accepting, understanding, but by no means approving of the ways of his people. Frankie Hannafey of *Come Back to Erin* evolves from revolutionary to ordinary citizen, yet is extraordinary in his honest confrontation with his country's and his own failures, leaving behind the imaginary for the real. Robert Younger of *And Again?* proves that life is worth living by doing it a second time, in reverse, making the same mistakes again and yet finding himself by doing precisely that.

It is hard to think of O'Faolain's short-story protagonists as heroes, but in many cases they do symbolize special life-visions which speak for the author himself, visions worthy of admiration.

One example is the symbolic protagonist of a later story, "Murder at Cobbler's Hulk,"[5] a retired travel agent with the ominous name of Bodkin. His formal courtesy is a throwback to the business world of the British Empire. Born in 1897 to a poor but respectable Anglo-Irish family, Bodkin served in impeccable anonymity at Tyrrell's Travel Agency in Dublin for nearly sixty years. That period spanned the Irish rebellion and its aftermath, times which Bodkin tolerated in his own way (when a client gave him a name "in the so-called Irish language," he would write down "Mr. Irish"). His uneventful life was not without thought or antagonism, and he planned and saved for a unique retirement to, of all places, an abandoned (first-class) railway car at Cobbler's Hulk, an obsolete station near the seaside village of Greystones. The characterization of Bodkin shows him to be more than an eccentric; he is a soul in rebellion against the tyrannies of history, prejudice, and ignorance as they have hampered his life.

Alone and near his carriage, he prays to the starry night:

> O Spirits, merciful and good! I know that our inheritance is held in store for us by Time. I know there is a sea of Time to rise one day, before which all who wrong us or oppress us will be swept away like leaves. I see it, on the flow! I know that we must trust and hope, and neither doubt ourselves nor doubt the good in one another. . . . O Spirits, merciful and good, I am grateful![6]

The fact that he is quoting Dickens does not lessen the impact of "those splendid radical words," nor does his prayer lessen our inclination to see Bodkin as an extension of O'Faolain's own feelings. On the surface, he is a nineteenth-century styled Englishman, but he is also in fact a throwback to the old-fashioned romantic revolutionary, totally independent. He is entirely misunderstood and underrated by his modern enemies, people like his vulgar boss at Tyrrell's, or pushy customers like old Lady Kilfeather.

His life has been suffered in silence, but in that silence he has been engaged in determined self-liberation. His retirement to his railway car symbolizes his intellectual revolution. Nearby live the very Irish Condons—Mary, Colm, and their aged mother. Bodkin befriends these poor people and loves them as his first true neighbors in a lonely life, and as substitutes for his own lost family. For the sake of the Condons, he becomes the "murderer" of Cobbler's Hulk.

Their happiness is threatened by a Lady Dobson, a wealthy Englishwoman who had formerly employed Colm as chauffeur and, in fact, as adulterous lover. In her destructive boredom, she has come seeking Colm to renew the affair, threatening the Condon's family harmony and independent life. Bodkin, who as travel agent had long and bitter experience with bored aristocrats, orchestrates Lady Dobson's destructive instincts upon herself, discouraging her in her pursuit of Colm and finally allowing her to drown within yards of his railway car outpost.

The "murder" reveals Bodkin as an all-out revolutionary against economic and moral oppression, yet he is entirely plausible as a representative of the common man's sufferings.

> Had he really felt oppressed? Or wronged? Could it be that, during his three years of solitude, he had been thinking that this would be a much nicer place if people did not go around shouting at one another or declaring to other people that time is money? Or wondering why Mother should have had to suffer shame and pain for years, while dreadful old women like Kilfeather went on scrounging, wheedling, bloodsucking, eating and drinking their way around this travelled world of which all he had ever seen was that dubious wink across the night sea?[7]

An aged man, Bodkin is another example of a personality's coming of age, or in this case, of the fruition of a lifetime of personality preparation for a crisis in justice. An unvanquished underdog, he alters the inhumanity of apparent fate by the power of his free mind. In fact, he becomes a symbol of mental freedom.

Bodkin is nevertheless an odd sort of avenger, a dynamic character with a conservative mask. It is rather characteristic of O'Faolain to create this ironical covering, and to make Bodkin's old-world manner interesting in its own right. O'Faolain's fascination for the human spectacle and its various life-modes is a creative quality that prevents his characters from being exploited as mere representations of ideas. The character has an air as well as a meaning, and the air can have a more lasting impression on the reader.

79

The character's mask is itself interesting, for it often works against the "message," qualifying it with an ironic resonance that is as representative of O'Faolain as the thematic idea.

O'Faolain entangles his own concerns into his characterizations without imposing his opinions upon them. The protagonist of the story "Teresa," a would-be nun, would-be saint, but in fact world-loving egotist, is a good example. O'Faolain's ideas about saintliness and sham saintliness are present in the story, but only by implication, and in no way insisted upon. He portrays Teresa on one level as a hypocrite, posing as a saint in a fit of adolescent vanity. Yet, he also makes her charming, a vivacious, mercurial character who can manipulate her reality when she finds it wanting in romance. She so passionately wears her saint-mask that she almost carries off the disguise, and the reader nearly forgets that she is motivated by outrageous egotism. But if we decide that because she is so motivated O'Faolain is simply satirizing the whole business of saintliness, we are missing a good deal of the story. Teresa is a flighty Irish girl, fascinated by her own changing image in a mirror. Though her actions seem inconsistent, she is always essentially herself, and her intensity challenges others to be more geniunely true to themselves. Two other characters in the story suggest actual rather than sham saintliness. The Godly Carmelite superioress is an impressive image of life beyond the human world. And in old Sister Patrick, Teresa's eclair-eating chaperone, O'Faolain depicts saintly goodness and humility in a worldy personality.

Through these characterizations O'Faolain clarifies both cloistered and profane worlds, yet shows them to be touching upon and even mixed into one another.

> They heard only the baby tongues of the waves. The evening star blazed in the russet sky. The old nun saw it, and she said, in part a statement, in part a prayer, in part a retort:
> "Sweet Star of the Sea!"
> Teresa raised her dark eyes to the star and she intoned in her girlish voice the poem of Saint Therese:
>> "Come, Mother, once again,
>> Who camest first to chide.
>> Come once again, but then
>> To smile—at eventide."
> The old nun fiddled with her beads. She drew long breaths through her nose. She tried several times to speak.

She gestured that they must go back. They turned and walked slowly back to the convent, side by side; the old nun as
restless as if she were in bodily agony, the novice as sedate
and calm as a statue. After a while Patrick fumbled in her
pocket, and found a chocolate, and popped it into her
mouth. Then she stopped chewing, and threw her eye at her
companion. At the look of intense sorrow in the face beside
her, she hunched up her shoulders and as silently as she
could, she gulped the fragments whole.[8]

Teresa's tendency to show up Patrick spoils the old nun's moments
of devotion and earthly pleasure, yet in her own mind Patrick will
not be outdone. She accepts life's plesures and devotes herself to
God. Though dramatically she seems mere comic foil to Teresa, she
is the one character in the story who is true to both worlds. In this
sense, Teresa can be considered comic foil to Patrick's essential
seriousness.

Her characterization matches a statement O'Faolain makes
about saintliness in *An Autumn in Italy*, when, after meeting the
famous Padre Pio, he writes:

Here is a truly saintly man. Thousands have spoken to him,
found him, as I did, kindly and jovial, amiable and kind,
and because his humanity is so evident his saintliness is all
the more impressive. For even if we do not say that this man
is a saint, nobody would find it difficult to believe that a
saint could be such a man.[9]

O'Faolain finds spirituality and mystery in human personality itself,
not in its trancendence. He believes in spirituality as an aspect of
physical life, and he searches for the eternal in human situations,
perceptions, and memories. He likes to look into and beyond the apparent contradictions of people, and he creates characters who embody apparent contradictions. The combination of absurdity and
seriousness that we see in a Bodkin or a Sister Patrick represents
O'Faolain's ironic yet sober vision of humanity. For him they are
part of both the spectacle and the meaning of life.

Unlike naturalistic writers, O'Faolain does not develop
characterization as an end in itself but rather as a means of in-
vestigating general humanity, general fate, and his own mind. In a

1934 essay criticizing the naturalistic novel, he states that the "analysis of character has gone too far," and he calls for a "greater sense of the poetry of life."[9] What he means is expressed more precisely in another essay on the same subject, published the following year.

> Men, when seen from a distance, are diminished certainly. But they are also glorified, being thereby restored to that dignity which belongs to the individual when he becomes part of a greater pageant than his own small life.[10]

This distancing is a way of creating characters with ambience, meaningful environments, and representative situations. The artist is not merely a psychologist; he is a conjurer of meaning through character. He can do so subtly, without didactic heaviness, as in the case of Chekhov's stories—an influence on O'Faolain's methods and tempermental outlook that is hard to overestimate. In *The Short Story*, he speaks of Chekhov's characterizations as a fulfillment of his own standards.

> No photographs, no absolute externality as of the Naturalists, then, for Chekov, and I find it the most admirable thing in him. He did say that he wished only to depict what he saw—but all writers say that, and he saw far more than most. Perhaps it is that he saw in his characters moments as well as men. That was the poet in him. He constantly wrought his people into situations that would satisfy this side of him, situations that opened little windows into their souls where they saw and confessed the mystery of a wider orbit of life than they or we commonly see, let alone admit, as we go about our daily trivialities.[11]

It is significant that O'Faolain speaks of "little windows" into the characters' souls, for, like Chekhov, he believes in subtlety and discretion in handling the spiritual life of characters, so that the causual aspect of actual life contains the mystery that is revealed in the story. Like Chekhov's, O'Faolain's stories are grounded in common life yet pivot upon moments of crisis in which the character's individual integrity is put on trial. The implications of the trial are universal.

"The Trout," a brief story of highly symbolic action, concerns a young girl, Julia, who in a single act of daring, rebellion, and yet responsibility, realizes her readiness for actual rather than imagined experience. Julia secretly leaves her bed one evening to rescue a pool-entrapped fish in a laurel grove. The grove is like a dark tunnel, even in the daytime, and she has always been a bit afraid while running through it. She is especially afraid to go into the tunnel at night, but she overcomes that fear and even dares to grasp the fish in its black pool and run with it to the river. It is an act of rebellion against her childhood morality and its protraction by her protective parents. In fact, when her mother tells her little brother a fairy tale about a "naughty fish who would not stay at home" to get his mind off the actual trapped fish, Julia protests, "Mummy, don't make it a horrible old moral story."[12] She has a passionate concern for the well-being of the real fish, and she realizes that no one else is going to save it. She obeys her self-imposed morality, turning away from the fairytale response, and becomes the trout's rescuer — an actual fairy godmother. Back in her bed after her secret adventure, she is delighted with herself: "She hugged herself and giggled. Like a river of joy her holiday spread before her."[13] She is as free as the swimming fish in her own life's river.

Julia's triumph is representative of a general human capacity for coming-of-age, with its attendant difficulties and rewards. The poetic imagery of the story is more memorable than her characterization, and she is part of that imagery of moonlight, dark path, a barefooted girl running over the stones, the silvery fish churning in the pitcher, the girl leaping into her bed, safe again. This domination of imagery and atmosphere distances the characterization, blending it into the symbolism of the story.

O'Faolain rightly considers himself a realist with a poetic purpose, a writer who uses the conventions of realism to create an illusion of reality while also conveying a personal way of seeing human existence. He wishes to reveal not only his subject but himself involved with it. He speaks of this aim in an essay entitled "Two Kinds of Novel."

> From the illusion there leaps whatever the novelist has in his heart to make leap. To use a loose word, some generalization emerges; not, indeed, some close-packed moral (Heaven forbid!); not even, of necessity, something capable of definition — rather an attitude, a characteristic mood, a sudden wash of color drawn across the landscape of experience. . . .
> [14]

Though often difficult to define, and seeming to be a happy accident, this personalized effect is certainly so of O'Faolain, who creates a fictional ambience which can be said to be his artistic signature. This is especially evident in his recreation of place, time, and cultural environment — elements that he handles uniquely.

"To describe scenery that a traveller can see with his own eyes is stupid."[15] O'Faolain makes this statement in *An Irish Journey*, one of his travel books. He could just as well be saying the same thing about his attitude toward fictional description; that is, why should he limit himself to mere eye-work? He believes that it is a part of the artist's task to imply his personality by his vision, and to do so in the interest of truth, not merely for an effect or for an ulterior motive. This belief is behind another comment he makes in a piece entitled "The Meaning of Place": "The nature of a man's response to place is a great test of his humanity. We can tell at once if he is pumping up the emotion, faking it . . . ."[16]The implication of this statement is that a geniune passion for setting is desirable in a writer, but that ulterior motives (he gives the examples of sentimentality and social conscience motives) deflect the mind from a genuine attachment and conception.

O'Faolain depicts his settings with the affectionate concern of a painter, yet he is in no way a descriptive decorator. While he is stylish and somewhat impressionistic in his descriptions of place, his imagery is always highly selective and thematically functional. Two examples of description of place illustrate this achievement.

The first, from the story "A Letter," concerns a young schoolmistress in a rural Irish town who longs for a fuller life elsewhere, but also responds to the charms of the country.

> At the top of the long slope she came out into the sun and saw the rocky landscape of the Commons spread out beneath her. It wavered under its own miasma. The little lake in the centre of it glinted all over. She turned off the road down her favourite boreen, wobbling intently between the cart-ruts, avoiding the overhanging briars that trailed lost threads of hay from the rank hedges on each side.
> The boreen wound and dropped until it came to an abrupt end at a gap stuffed with furze bushes. There she threw her bicycle into a hedge and drank from the icy well,

noticing how the dribbling water dried on the flagstone. She
delayed to admire the line of poplars beyond. She looked for
the distant spire of the village. It was so pale that it was
almost invisible. She clambered over the gap and thrust
through the scrub that borders the lake until she came on
open water between tall reeds. She crunched forward on the
strand, dazzled by the whiteness of its minute crustacea.
When she lay down the water glittered level with her eye.[17]

The imagery seems as casual as if it were dashed upon a canvas, and
yet it is as precise and essential in its detail as a Frost poem about
country moods in a solitary being. This is exactly what the story is
about. When the young woman looks for the spire, we sense that she
has been in this place before, that it is of special significance to her,
and that she is seeking some part of herself. These are all functional
effects in the story's main line. But the imagery epitomizes more
than her mood; it symbolizes rural Ireland in high summer, the time
of O'Faolain's own chidhood memories of Limerick. The hazy
distances suggest memory, while the closeups — like the drops of
water on the flagstone — suggest magnified contemplation. When
the schoolmistress lies down level with lake water the moment seems
to represent an archetypal return to earth of the exiled heart, not
just her own troubled heart but every Irishman's, including
O'Faolain's. This dissatisfied girl is giving her affections a chance to
restore her to the ground, at least for a healing moment. She is
visiting her Innisfree, though knowing that she cannot live there.
The ironic upshot of this episode is that she later returns to her
frustrations, which in fact feed upon the inarticulate beauty around
her.

This complex of emotion, its universal application, and
O'Faolain's own involvement with it, are not merely supported by
descriptive passages like this but emerge out of them. The descriptions contain the theme.

The provincial motif that is present in "A Letter" is everywhere
in O'Faolain's fiction, even in his descriptions of towns and
townspeople, for the open country edges his Irish towns, and a peasant conservatism persists in their inhabitants.

The second example of a descriptive passage is the opening of a
later story, 'Hymeneal,'' which depicts a residential part of Dublin

where two ageing couples live in middle-class comfort and respectability.

> Away back in 1929, a few months before they got married,
> Phil and Abby Doyle had bought a red-and-yellow brick
> house, semi-detached, with a small garden in front and a
> useful strip for vegetables at the rear, on the North Circular
> Road. It stood about halfway between the Dublin Cattle
> Market and the entrance to the Phoenix Park — to be precise
> a bare 1300 feet, or 80 perches, from the park Gate, as Phil
> had once carefully established in his schoolmasterish way by
> means of a pedometer attached to his left leg. All in all it
> was a pleasant quarter, so convenient to the city that Abby
> could be down in O'Connell Street by tram within ten
> minutes, and yet sufficiently remote for almost unbroken
> quietness. On still summer nights she could sometimes hear
> the morose growling of lions from the Zoological Gardens,
> the crazed laughter of monkeys. Early in the morning, if the
> wind was from the east, she might hear the mooing of cattle
> and the baaing of sheep from the Market. Otherwise the on-
> ly obtrusive noise was when an occasional freight train from
> Kingsbridge came trundling along the loop north of the city
> down to the quays and the cargo steamers for England. But
> the greatest attraction of the North Circular for Abby was
> that when her sister Molly married Failey Quigley in the
> following year, they had bought an identical house next
> door.[18]

Here is a vision of a planned, utilitatian, orderly life. Abby,
who seems most content with it, is the dominant figure in the
passage. And yet, what the story reveals is a frustrated romance between Abby and Failey, and the lifelong confidence that they shared
as mutual supporters of their two unromantic marriages. This
revelation is further masked by O'Faolain's choice of the rather im-
perceptive and boorish Phil as the dominant point of view character
in the story. It is he who discovers the true essence of their lives while
looking through the deceased Failey's papers. The passage quoted
above that opens the story acts as a mask for this revelation, but it
also contains subtle keys to its unlocking. The passage's implicit
characterizations prepare us for the complex human relationships to
be revealed, all signalled through a description of the
neighborhood. We learn that "schoolmasterish" Phil had selected

the unassuming house before their marriage, in effect chartering out Abby's life in his measured, practical, obtuse way. We also discover that Abby likes that life's convenience, quietude, and its suggestion of a mercantile atmosphere mixed with a hint of the agrarian. Abby's acceptance of Phil's proposal of marriage was a romantic tragedy for her, but it was also a ready acquiescence to her conservative instincts. Her life with Phil seemed fated once he took the trouble to propose. Given her humble expectations, she felt she could not expect to indulge her own desires. The cries of the imprisoned zoo animals do not disturb her, and she takes consolation in Failey's marriage to her sister and in their next-door nearness. Though Phil becomes a tiresome and insensitive husband, Abby ultimately decides that the daily round of life on the North Circular Road is good. It is on this note that the opening description rests.

This opening passage reveals enough of Abby's mentality to imply why such hidden lives are lived and how the consolation of trivial satisfactions becomes life itself. The commonplace details of Abby's neighborhood and her attitude toward them make up a fascinating vision of the complex balancing act that is modern middle-class life, aware of its mediocrity yet generally untroubled by it, clinging to its small pleasures of convenience, its air of mobility and variety, and its sense of being in touch with the general progress.

"All in all it was a pleasant quarter," writes O'Faolain, interjecting his ironic but understanding voice. Yes, one can imagine a better, more beautiful, more fulfilling condition; but yes again, it *was* in its way pleasant for a woman like Abby to live in such a place, at such a time, and under such a cultural umbrella. In *Vive Moi!* O'Faolain makes a similar qualification in recalling a schoolteacher nicknamed Doggy, dull but loyal, hard-working and kind.

> Doggy was a drudge, but not a sad drudge. It is one definition of insanity to have an itch, and of sanity to have a niche. He had made his own modest image of himself. He had found a niche in the city's body politic to enshrine it. So much of life is a pure act of the imagination![19]

This last statement reveals that side of O'Faolain that refuses to condescend, that seeks and finds value in the least likely places and people. It is this enthusiasm that animates his descriptive writing, making his creative relationship to his subject apparent.

O'Faolain's fascination with the ambience of place is one of his most romantic qualities. The external world is there for his eager discovery. The same can be said of his endless curiosity about the relativity of time in the human mind and about the mysteries of memory. In this latter case, he would consider himself typically Irish. "Time and memory!" he exclaims in an article entitled "Dyed Irish," "They are the two main inspirations of the Irish imagination."[20] Benedict Kiely considers him one of the most no-stalgic of Irish writers, though a rebel against Irish sentimentality.[21] O'Faolain is unique in that his nostalgia is useful to him; he treats it, to use one of his own aesthetic phrases, as a stimulant, not a drug. His distant associations do render an aura to his dramatic moments, but he does not leave the reader with aura alone.

Usually the question "why?" makes an entrance, as in the case of the already discussed Daniel Cashen of "A Touch of Autumn in the Air."

> The illuminating thing was the bewildered look that came into those pale, staring eyes as he talked. It revealed that he was much more touched and troubled by the Why of memory than the Fact of memory. He was saying, in effect: Why do I remember that? Why do I not remember the other thing?[22]

O'Faolain seeks "the illuminating thing" in time passage and memory, the revelation of a truth through distancing and wide association. In an essay called "Romance and Realism," he remarks: "In twilight, in memory, in age, and in exile, Ireland is at her loveliest and most indubitable."[23] I think most of this statement is representative of the Irish imagination, but that the last three words characterize O'Faolain especially. He believes that a truth can be found in the maze of a remembering personality, that illumination underlies our human confusion as we reencounter the past.

It follows that one of his major artistic missions is to capture moments when fresh experience and memory intersect, revealing emotional depths and conjuring up meanings. Often his characters are assailed by their pasts as they try to progress in their lives. Some, more fatalistic, try to locate their destinies by seeking their pasts. The opening paragraph of "The Patriot" concerns the latter case.

88

> It was doubtless because of the inevitable desire of man to recapture the past that they went to Youghal for their honeymoon. Their friends expected them to go at least to Dublin, if not to London or Paris, but they both knew in their hearts that they had spent the gayest days of their lives in this little town, and so as if to crown all those early happinesses to Youghal they went, like true voluptuaries deliberately creating fresh memories that would torment them when they were old.[24]

To romantics like the lovers in this story, remembered life is a shrine to which they make pilgrimage; they desire to recapture the past or at least to be deeply affected by it. Such pilgrimages become a kind of religion of personality. In "The Patriot," O'Faolain sets a romantic love affair in opposition to the idealism of romantic revolution, revealing a similar greed in both for remembered moments, enshrined myths. It is one of his most Irish traits to reveal the intensity of conflicts between mythologies, be they personal or public.

"Discord," a story of young married lovers encountering an antiquarian priest in Dublin, is similar in conflict and theme to "The Patriot."[25] These lovers believe in their power to recreate themelves over and over in lovemaking. The priest, a solitary, seeks his imaginative satisfactions in the study of historical Dublin. Lovers and priest are shown to be incompatible and uncomfortable with each other, not merely for the institutions they represent, nor for the lovers' physicality and the priest's intellectuality, but because they wish to pursue different pasts and to create different beliefs out of that pursuit.

Masked by his characters and their situations, O'Faolain's own mythologized past is his main subject as a writer. Their memories and obsessions are slightly displaced versions of his own. The places that affect their lives are the places that have affected his. His many fictional recreations of the city of Cork can serve as an example of his handling of place and time as an extension of himself. The remembered Cork of his youth and the revisited Cork of his maturity are psychological landscapes of his experience, uniquely expressed in his art.

His first three novels, *A Nest of Simple Folk*, *Bird Alone*, and *Come Back to Erin*, are to a large extent personal interpretations of his native city. There are about twenty Cork stories, not including the several West Cork rural tales.

For O'Faolain, the spirit of Cork is self-contradictory or paradoxical; it is shabby but beautiful, witty and tough-minded but sinister and smug, dream-inspiring but dream-denying. It is a place for an artist to be born in, to remember, but most of all to escape from. These characteristics and their effect on him are the real subject underlying the Cork tales. I categorize them into three main types: tales of claustrophobia, of dissent, and of revisitation.

In the claustrophobic Cork tales, the characters seem destined to stay or return there foreever, caught in the city's ageing tendrils. They may or may not realize the completeness of their confinement, but the writer does, and generates his fear of it. These tales concern half-hearted and doomed revolts against the city's ethos. Examples are "The Old Master," concerning a revolt in taste of a ballet enthusiast against the militant censorship of O'Faolain's remembered Cork; "A Born Genius,"[26] regarding the revolt in ambition of a talented singer in a Philistine environment; and "One Man, One Boat, One Girl," concerning a sexual rebellion against the marriage-religion alliance.

This latter story, from *The Heat of the Sun*, has a young and conventional Corkman as narrator, Alphonsus, who barely understands the conflicts he is witness to. He shares a temporary bachelor life of illicit pursuit of women with another young man, Olly Carson, and an ageing antifeminist, T.J. Mooney. T.J.'s fear of the moral domination of women and priests is expressed in violent eloquence.

> "All every woman is waiting for is the day she can lay you
> out and be praying for you, and feeling good about you.
> They keep you out of their bed when you're alive, and they
> sleep with you when you're dead."[27]

T.J.'s diatribe, poured into the narrator's confused ears, is his angry response to the death and funeral of Olly, whose pietistic wife, Janey Anne Breen, had indeed made a holy symbol of her once free-wheeling husband.

> T.J. and me went down to the house for the funeral and she
> brought us in to see him in the coffin. When I saw what I

saw the tears started rolling down my face. She had him laid out in the Franciscan habit, and at his head she had laid the little Papal flag that used to stand in the vase on her side of the mantelpiece. I never saw any woman look so happy.[28]

Janey Anne's smug self-assurance makes T.J.'s vitriolic personality seem humane, and the story ends with a sympathetic vision of him on the River Lee, seen there through the eyes of the now respectably and fearfully married Alphonsus.

For years I did not lay eyes on him, until last month when I was walking down the marina one Sunday with Fan pushing little Sean in the gocart, and I had Dierdre on my shoulder. Suddenly I stopped dead. I saw the gray-haired man on the river, pulling along at his ease. In the prow with her nose up was a red setter, and it was that made me recognize him.
"Fan!" I said. "That's T.J."
"She looked and she laughed sharplike.
"The Rule of the River," she said.
It was a lovely June morning, wind from the southwest, and the ebb with him. Very nice. He would come back on the tide. As late as he liked.
"Well?" Fan asked. "What are you thinking?"
"Ach! Nothing!"
"You were smiling," she said suspiciously.
"Was I?"
"Yes, you were!" she said and she gave me a dark look.
"I was just smiling sadlike. Thinking what a lonely poor divil he is."
We walked on. I watched him slowly pull away from us. I could not get the old barcarolle out of my head.
"River girls, O river girls. How we love your dancing curls" . . .
I was very careful not to smile.[29]

In this moment O'Faolain recaptures the Cork that he has called "a bore, and a bitch, and a beauty,"[30] the Cork of narrow-mindedness, of the challenging sneer, and of romantic longing that colored his own youth.

In the Cork tales of dissent, rebels or nonconformists living within the body politic achieve some measure of success as partakers of life's pleasures. They succeed by internally defying the moral or intellectual order, ignoring the pressures of conformity. Examples are "Billy Billee," a memory-tale about a childhood friendship with a loose woman; "Vive la France,"[31] about the Irish yearning for foreign places; and "Thieves,"[32] about the predawn escapades of two children in the Cork lanes.

"Billy Billee" is narrated by an old writer recalling the first stirrings of amorous desire and literary emotion while looking through some sixty-year-old papers. Among them he finds his first penny catechism, which sets off a memory of his fourteenth-year friendship with Lottie Black (Billy Billee). She was a fleshy, middle-aged artiste of the music halls, an Englishwoman who boarded at the boy's home during her performances at the old Cork Opera House. The boy Jacky became enamored of her perfumed, frilled room, with its photos of fleshy dancers and its trinkets of her travelled life. He became her confidant, for his adolescent yearning was a match for her undying life-lust. Against this relationship (a kind of love affair) stood joy-denying, provincial Cork, Lottie's loveless marriage, and the boy's adolescent limitations. What Jacky learned from Lottie, however, was that there could be pleasure in what was considered sinful by his culture—not just physical pleasure, but long-lasting pleasure of the imagination. This pleasure, the old writer realizes, overcomes the denying forces of poverty, ignorance, age (at both extremes), and intolerance. The individual human spirit can arm itself against all. He also recognizes how Lottie struggled with those forces, symbolized by his remembered image of her gazing out her lace-curtained window at Cork's human traffic. In gratefulness to her humanity, he composes a celebratory "Ballad of Billy Billee," and inscribes it in his sixty-year-old catechism. "Billy Billee" is clearly a version of O'Faolain's childhood in the house on Half-Moon Street, placed, its seems by destiny, between the "double doors" of Saint Peter's and St. Paul's Church and the Cork Opera House.

In the Cork stories that I call revisitation tales, escaped Corkmen return and in effect tend to their unfinished pasts, but are able to detach themselves enough to go free again. They also have enought perspective to glimpse the meaning of Cork, and to realize that meaning as part of themselves. Examples are "Up the Bare Stairs," about how a childhood humiliation makes a man both a success and an exile; "Dividends," concerning types of wish-fulfillment in maturity and later life; and "The Kitchen," about time's erosion of the things people value most.

"Dividends" may be O'Faolain's most representative story, for it contains a great number of his most prominent motifs, and combines his mature, ironical tonality with an evocation of the ways of his past. It begins with a trainride down to Cork from Dublin, an experience that Sean, the narrator, likens to Orpheus's descent. O'Faolain's trainrides are usually journeys into someone's past, and in this case he does not disguise the fact that it is his own past that he is looking into. His persona returns to two Corks, however, one modern and one antique. Modern Cork is represented by his old friend, Mel Meldrum, an ageing but sporting bachelor who runs a stock brokerage, drives a fast Jaguar car, keeps a modern suburban bungalow, and pursues a handsome young woman — his housemaid — with suave confidence. Antique Cork is represented by the narrator's old Aunt Anna Whelan, a retired housekeeper now ensconced in a tenement on Lavitt's Quay. Sean returns to straighten out the old woman's paltry but confused economic affairs, for she has withdrawn her small shares from one of Meldrum's stocks, yet insists that he keep paying her her monthly "divvies." Anna considers her little dividends a form of status achieved after a lifetime of want.

The idea of dividends is also metaphoric of the dream-life of Mel Meldrum and his housemaid, Shiela. Mel, nearing fifty, is grooming Shiela to be his dream-mate, a fine dividend for all his years of celibate abstinence. Shiela, a poor girl, is temporarily drawn to the comforts of Mel's wealth, dividends for her patient investment of her beauty.

Though Sean tries to encourage Mel in his pursuit of Shiela, his visit reminds Mel of his advancing age; meanwhile, Anna's lack of realism troubles Mel with misgivings about his own romanticism. He begins to feel that he is too old for Shiela, and gives her up because he is afraid to risk his happiness with her. This is another withdrawal of shares in conservative Cork style; he even hires old Anna as his new housemaid — a guard against temptation.

Sean leaves Cork through the long train tunnel, sniffing "the rancid smell of the underworld," escaping from Cork's stagnation as he did as a young man.

> For that mile of tunnel I had them all there together with me in that dark carriage, with the cold smell of steam, and an occasional splash of water on the roof from the ventila-

tion shafts to the upper air. Abruptly, the tunnel shot away, and I felt like a skin diver soaring from the sea to the light of day. Green country exploded around me on all sides in universal sunlight. Small, pink carts went ambling below me along dusty side roads to the creamery. Black and white cows munched. Everywhere in the fields men were at their morning work. I opened the window to let in the fresh air.[33]

O'Faolain's spiritual flight from the stagnation and confinement of the past is symbolized here, as it is elsewhere in his work, by imagery of Cork and the country beyond it, of darkness and light, of stillness and movement, of water and air. It is no accident that his Cork settings are often dark, still, and watery; for in his mythic memory, Cork is a city under the sea of time.

O'Faolain calls himself a "romantic with a hopeless longing for classical order," one who attempts to tame "despotic fact" by subjecting it to form.[34] Such an attempt is romantic in itself. The realization of that attempt's actual futility is realistic in the extreme. O'Faolain recognizes the limits of the power of personality, yet totally commits himself to the personality's needs through imaginative improvisation. This is not art for art's sake, but art for self's sake. O'Faolain would consider the artist's primary responsibility to be to tend to himself, to put his own personality in order. He is a romantic realist.

He has written of modern writers' problems with the apparent meaninglessness of a morally indifferent and anti-individualist age, and has expressed his fear of "the death of personality" by self-deception, evasion of challenge, and yielding to external force.[35] Yet, he sees modern life as meaningful, though generally subject to great uncertainty, disorder, and disaffection. These human problems increase his curiosity about his own times. Though the age may seem chaotic, he looks to his own growth of personality through difficult times and experiences, and is hopeful. His own life is a model for his fictional themes, and much of his fiction is disguised and dramatized autobiography. He consistently implies that the most important art is the art of personality—a confrontation of the external choas by means of a poised, self-possessing internal order. One may not be able to overcome external forces, or to significantly remake one's world, but it is still possible to pursue one's own ends.

A story that seems to symbolize this attitude is "The End of the Record," a fictionalization of the death of Ansty, Tailor Tim Buckley's widow. The story concerns a visit by a folklorist and a radio technician to a poorhouse in western Ireland, where they meet the crazed and dying Mary Creegan of West Cork. The two men wish to collect stories from the old people, as one inmate tells another:

> "And they say that he would give you a five-shilling piece into your hand for two verses of an old song," said Thomas Hunter, an old man from Coomacoppal, in West Kerry, forgetting that five-shilling peices were no longer in fashion. "Or for a story, if you have a good one."
>
> "What sort of stories would them be?" Michael Kivlehan asked sceptically. He was from the barony of a Forth and Bargy, in County Wexford, and had been in the poorhouse for eleven years.
>
> "Any story at all only it is to be an old story and a good story. A story about the fairies, or about ghosts, or about the way people lived long ago."
>
> "And what do he do with 'um when he have 'um?"
>
> "Hasn't he a phonograph? And doesn't he give them out over the wireless? And doesn't everyone in Ireland be listening to them?"[36]

This Synge-like exchange is very rare in O'Faolain's fiction; his use of Irish country dialect is usually limited to a random phase or a line from a song. Here he uses it to set a tone at the beginning of the story, one that is more pathetic than comical, though certainly a mixture of both. Thomas and Michael disappear from the story after this exchange, their brief conversation acting as an overture to the story of Mary Creegan's last moments. What O'Faolain is doing is depicting folk-Ireland going silent, ironically happening at the peak moment of official interest in the fading culture. The world of the folk can no more be bribed back into existence than can a five-shilling piece buy happiness. But the collector asks for a ghost story from Mary, and she, something of a ghost herself, complies by telling a tale of a dying renegade priest who is refused a last confession by the parish priest. In the style of a moral fable, Mary comments, "And that was a hard thing to do, for no man should refuse the dying."

When the reader considers that it is she, the storyteller, who is dying, the story takes on a symbolic significance. Mary tells how the candles by the dying priest are miraculously lit by invisible hands, signalling his salvation in spite of the parish priest. In this theme is a suggestion of Mary's own salvation under her own code of values, and she sees what she calls "a great brightness" before falling into a faint. The sympathetic doctor leads the collector away with fatalistic words: "When that generation goes it will be all over."

No one can recapture the quality of mind that is Mary's, but the collector stops his truck to play back the recording of her ghost story. The two men hear her words again, including her final statement about seeing a great brightness.

> The listeners relaxed. Then from the record came a low, lonely cry. It was the fluting of a bittern over moorland. It fluted sadly once again, farther away, farther away; and for a third time, almost too faint to be heard.[37]

They play it back several times, needing to be convinced that the bird cry is real. Each time it sounds its wail of the mountains.

The story, which begins with the pathetic comedy of old Thomas and Michael, ends on this ghostly and elegaic note. The world has left Mary Creegan and her kind behind; but, in a way, she has outshone that world. The pathetic note is qualified by a sense of her nobility, for she dies like an old peasant woman of West Cork, not merely like any other ward of the poorhouse. The cry of the bittern seems almost supernatural, suggesting a mysterious salvation. For Mary, the world of ghosts and miracles and mountain life goes on forever, though for the rest of the world it is in fact "all over."

Like Yeats before him, O'Faolain cuts away at the conventions that separate the romantic and the ironic. In a way, he is speaking for himself as an artist when he has Mary Creegan answer the question of whether or not she believes in the ghosts: "I do *not* believe in 'um. But they're there."[38] Those memorable words are a cheerful expression of the human capacity to live in both scepticism and imagination, to allow oneself to see clearly and yet feel deeply. To deny a creative person either outlet would be wrong.

O'Faolain does not simply undercut romantic feeling by means of ironic realism. Each element qualifies and in a sense verifies the other. The romantic and the ironic are like intertwining strands in O'Faolain's fiction; they disappear behind one another only to reemerge, overlap, and disappear again.

A case for illustration is the ironically entitled tale, "How to Write a Short Story," from the late collection, *Foreign Affairs and Other Stories*. Its two main characters generally represent youthful romanticism and mature irony, yet the older character emerges as a romantic figure by story's end. Young Morgan Myles and ageing Frank Breen (I have already mentioned their appearance in "Falling Rocks, Narrowing Road, Cul-de-sac, Stop") are librarian and doctor in a provincial Irish town, bachelors who support each other in their eccentricities. They are drawn from the actual friendship between the young writer-librarian, Frank O'Connor, and the ageing scholar-physician, Richard Hayes. On an evening visit, Myles notices a photograph of a beautiful boy, which turns out to be a picture of sixty-year-old Frank Breen at the age of twelve. Myles, a fanatical romantic who has decided to channel his abundant energies into writing realistic short stories, "to out-Maupassant Maupassant," demands a revelation of the loves that such a boyish face had inspired. He gets more Maupassant realism than he bargained for, for Breen surprises him with a memory of a homosexual experience that happened to him when he was that attractive child, a boarder at a Catholic boys' school in England.

The school leader, a boy six years older, became enamoured of his beauty and adopted him as a pet. Young Frank returned his attentions with naive hero-worship. Myles, hearing this much, begins to interpret the story as an idyll of innocent love when Breen, who has never gotten over the experience, cuts him short.

> "You think so?" the doctor said morosely. "I think he was going through hell all that year. At eighteen? On the threshold of manhood? In love with a child of twelve? That is, if you will allow that a youth of eighteen may suffer as much from love as a man twenty years older."[39]

Breen sympathizes with his first lover, who died soon after leaving school. He thinks of him as a victim of confused maturation and unnatural repression rather than as a perverse seducer. And yet the older boy did seduce Frank, who took gallant risks to be with his hero while being ignorant of his sexual motives. Myles, on the other hand, covers his eyes while listening to the gross details of the child's molestation, and sympathizes with that abused child, young Frank. The worst part of the affair, however, was the cover up, orchestrated by the priests, who, terrified of scandal, inculcated a guilty repression in Frank.

Myles listens to this sequel with indignation, cursing life as "a trollop," while at the same time blessing art as the "one fountain of truth, one beauty, one perfection." The doctor's ironical answer to this romantic platitude, "It is a view,"[40] undercuts the ostensible romanticism of the younger writer, a man too eager for intensity. Myles seeks inspiration by formula and turns up as the comic butt in the story. Yet the story itself turns out to be more lyrical than ironical in its totality.

For all his irony, Frank Breen's first love turns out to have been the most intense love of his life, though it made him a victim of cruel seduction. Seen through Breen's sympathetic memory, the seducer also emerges as a tragic being, destined to die before his confused passions could right themselves. Breen's sympathy turns the story from merely being a satire on Myles's besotted romanticism into a genuine expression of deep loneliness, fated to some by the trauma that is first love. The story tells us that life is not just a trollop. It is as painfully romantic as it is ironic.

By uniting the romantic and the ironic, by balancing these two extremes in his nature, O'Faolain produces delicate effects. His humor, one of his most enduring aspects, is also a balancing mechanism. In *Short Stories: A Study in Pleasure*, he writes that humor "is, to me, essentially the result of a deep-rooted longing for a sense of proportion."[41] Humor can be an adjustment to too much pessimism; it can also be a corrective to too much idealism.

One story that illustrates both kinds of humor is the long tale, "In the Bosom of the Country," from the 1963 collection, *The Heat of the Sun*. Like many of O'Faolain's most comic tales, this one turns on the head of the Irish Catholic needle, portraying two adulterous lovers in middle age. Frank Keene and Anna Mohan have been lovers for ten years, the same period in which Frank, an Englishman and a retired army major, has been living in Ireland. The story begins in the adulterous bed; a phone call reports the death of Arty Mohan, Anna's husband. At the point of sinking of its own weight, the affair takes on a new dimension because of this death: now it is possible for the "lovers" to be married.

Frank attends the funeral and notes that "the Irish have a great gift for death, wakes and funerals. They are really at their best in misfortune."[42] His comfortable alienation is shaken when he finds that Anna not only wishes to marry him but also to see him converted to her Catholic faith.

> "This," he declared, "is a bomb-shell. Dammit, it's an absolute bomb-shell. When we couldn't marry you were so afraid to lose me that you never uttered a word about religion, and now, when we can marry, you give me the choice of being a cad if I don't and a Catholic if I do."[43]

Either prospect is distasteful to him. He is a loyal, gentlemanly lover who is dismayed to find in Anna the common Irish Catholic eagerness to make converts for the old Faith. The irony is that she is in every other way a very lax Catholic.

O'Faolain's humor pivots on both the satiric and the life-affirming sides of the situation. Anna's evangelical pose is handled satirically, as is Frank's conversion. Yet that conversion turns out to be humorous in a warm-hearted way—an illustration of how a man of good will, albeit an adulterer and a man of the world, procedes.

Frank's journey into the bosom of the country includes a marvelously witty encounter with an old army priest, who, in giving him religious instruction appeals to his sense of fellowship, orderliness, and good taste more than to his soul. It may be, however, that these humane qualities *are* Frank's soul.

At first he is troubled by every oddity of Catholicism.

> "Mixed marriages, for instance. There's another tall order. And let me see, hasn't there been some difficulty about the Virgin? And then, of course, there's contraception—ran into that a lot in India. I need hardly say my interest in the matter is purely academic."
>
> "So is mine."
>
> He rose.
>
> "Why don't you come to dinner next week, Major, when as you say you will have thought some more about it,

and we can combine business, if I may so call it, with pleasure. I've got quite a sound port."[44]

Here is a perfect priest for Major Frank Keene, calm, tactful, understanding, and refined. I believe O'Faolain likes him as much as Frank does. The upshot of this relationship is that Frank becomes an enthusiastic Catholic, marries Anna, and drives her balmy with his soldierly obedience to Church law, law that Anna has never troubled herself about.

It takes time and the death of the old army priest to convert him over to her kind of Catholicism, gratifying but undemanding. The story ironically ends the way it began, with the married couple loafing late in bed on a Sunday morning, and getting up for bacon and coffee, but not mass. This ending combines religious satire with creative humor. Though they are poor practicing Catholics, Frank and Anna have made several successful adjustments to their personalities and their relationship. They are so content that they even accept the fact that they are living in the bosom of the country, respectable sinners of Ireland.

This story, like most of O'Faolain's comic fiction, stops short of farce, for he does not wish to evade the dark implications of the reality presented. Yet comedy of this sort does soften the blow of brutal life. O'Faolain shows us how we are *in fact* comical. We live in our imaginations whenever reality allows. Our evasions are at best partially and temporarily successful, yet they, as well as the grim things we evade, are out lives. O'Faolain's comic vision is his most complete vision.

CHAPTER FOUR

Extensions of Irishness

In a review of *Vive Moi!* Maurice Harmon remarks that O'Faolain's autobiography can be read as a record of twentieth-century Irish life, suggesting that O'Faolain's maturation, like that of other writers of his generation, parallels his country's evolution into independence.[1] O'Faolain is a representative Irishman in both his life and his art. His experiences exemplify recent Irish social history in several ways. Born of a poor, Catholic, working-class family that had close ties to an agrarian past, raised at the tail-end of the British colonial era in Ireland, touched by Gaelic revivalism as a youngster, drawn into the chaos of political revolution and civil war as a young man, returned to prosaic earth after the Troubles, hardened by a period of exile and foreign education, caught up in the social conflicts of the DeValera era, granted long life and a long look at the modern evolution of the Irish people, O'Faolain's life seems an essentialization of the modern Irish experience.

He is representative as a writer in several ways. His work is rooted in the literature of his elders, the progenitors or the Irish Literary Renaissance, yet is part of his own generation's distinct development. His latter career ties itself into the contemporary literature of Ireland and helps to give it direction and definition. A prose writer with poetic talent and taste, an analytic viewer of the Irish scene who experienced the romantic era of Irish nationality, he

101

stands, both by destiny of temperament and accident of history, at the crossroads of modern Irish aesthetics. He encompasses the breadth of modern Irish literary themes in his fiction and analytic writing, clarifying the familiar Irish subjects of town and country, faith and freedom, family and isolation, nationalism and aestheticism, exile and return, poverty and revolution, memory and desire.

He is not a museum-piece writer, however. He extends the validity of these subjects by showing them to be more various, distinctive, and modern than we had suspected. His uniqueness rests on his continuous contemporaneity, a sense of newness that is most apparent in his imagery, characterization, and character situations. He shows us old Ireland changing into new Ireland, the many ways of being Irish, and convinces us that the Irish identity is no longer knowable through the old cliches.

As I have suggested, O'Faolain's admiration and understanding of the writers of the previous Irish generation helped him to find his own way as an artist. In general, he felt that they had graced the Irish scene with an inspiring example of creative individuality. In the manner and matter of their personalities and writings, they were often influential upon him. That influence became less apparent as he matured, but it remained in the grain of his work.

In "Fifty Years of Irish Literature," a 1942 *Bell* editorial, O'Faolain speaks with his usual admiration of Yeats's creative personality. He particularly admires Yeats's ability to contain a "varied and complex" intellectualism through the power of creative affections.

> He could reconcile . . . a love of French Symbolistic poetry with an equal love for Gaelic folklore, which seems like reconciling the Remote with the Intimate. He did it through the idea that the most simple things became symbols by long and familiar association, and so evoke emotions that become precise while remaining indefinable. He would develop that idea until he left one convinced that the step from the intimate to the immense was the only possible progression in literature . . . .[2]

This kind of Yeatsian idealism was extremely influential on O'Faolain and the younger Irish writers of the 1930s. The familiar

Ireland was more than simply the proper subject for them; it was, as Yeats taught, the entryway to intense feeling and therefore to the highest kind of poetry.

Though Yeats's view of the familiar was so indirect and idiosyncratic as to make his Irish reality seem a mythological dream, his desire to evoke poetic symbols out of common life was taken up by young fiction-writers like O'Faolain, O'Flaherty, and O'Connor. They sought poetic evocation through a realistic handling of the familiar. They wished to match Yeats's creative exaltation, though they saw their world in a Chekhovian rather than a Shellean manner. For them, the step from the intimate to the immense was a less heroic matter; the artist did not soar but descended to ground level in his creation.

O'Faolain speaks of Yeats's love of the exceptional in "Fifty Years of Irish Literature."

> For he loved all that was remote and uncommon and
> "distinguished and lonely," saw the element of nobility in
> the simplest people, and never allowed his affection for the
> familiar to be confused with a surrender to the popular.[3]

This wide-ranging love of nobility for its own sake was not typical in Irish writing after Yeats. The idea of the noble peasant continued to exist as a kind of national sentiment, but not with the aesthetic value Yeats had invested in it. His view of the nobility of the artist's calling *did* have a strong effect on the younger writers, who often followed his example by courageously confronting popular opposition or public censure. A few, such as Liam O'Flaherty, had a definite heroic aesthetic, stressing courageous individualism in their work.

O'Faolain, however, is exceptionally close to Yeats in appreciating the presence of nobility at all levels of life and seeking a potential for it in human integrity. He adopts the Yeatsian notion of unity-of-being early in his career, and it becomes part of his maturing vision. Where Yeats magnifies individualism and makes it dramatic, O'Faolain focuses on the difficult birth of individuality in ordinary life. Though the modulation is different, both artists see individuality as the result of a noble struggle with the world and the self.

This Yeatsian aspect of personality fulfillment shows itself strongly in O'Faolain's first novel, *A Nest of Simple Folk*. He begins by counterpointing the protagonist, Leo Foxe-Donnel, with his

103

more commonplace relatives. Leo is more obstinate than integrated as a personality, and in this regard he is very much like O'Flaherty's novelistic heroies—crude, courageous, but not terribly self-aware. His struggle is with his cultural environment and social world, not with himself; he is mentally incomplete. It is partially to suggest this unrealized potential in Leo that O'Faolain brings young Denis Hussey into the latter part of the novel. Denis is the son of Johnny Hussey, Leo's nephew and antithetical spirit. Leo, a revolutionary, and Johnny, a sergeant in the Royal Irish Constabulary, are political and emotional enemies, the uncle prodigal, the nephew conservative in every way. Denis is an internalization of the family conflict. He is also an initiate individual, a boy who chooses his grand-uncle's way over his father's.

By understanding both ways, by recognizing them as parts of himself, and by choosing between them, Denis is an advance in personality over the blindly brave Leo. When he sees old Leo and his companions going off to fight and die in the Easter Rising in Dublin, we are presented with a powerful image of the old man's courage.

> He was about to turn home when he saw a motor-car standing by the kerb, down the farther road where it debouched, through cement-plastered villas, on the world of fields and hedges. A familiar figure was clambering into it—his Uncle Leo. For a moment the blood pounded into his heart. Then he saw John O'Donnell. Another man climbed in to the wheel, and he knew too—it was Jeremiah Haugh, the bookmaker. A fourth man came out of the house with a long and seemingly heavy parcel under his arm, and he knew him, too. It was Bwoala Maowara. He laid the parcel heavily in the back seat, and then got in beside it himself. Seeing him there with these hunted men he ceased to be an uncouth clodhopper of an Irish teacher, and became, of a sudden, large, ominous, powerful bodied—a man to be feared.[4]

There is a touch of Yeats's "Easter, 1916" about this scene, the everyday motley transforming itself into history. Yet this picture of revolutionary insurgence is coventional when compared to the scene that precipitates Denis's revolt against his father, home, and former self. In that episode, Denis articulates his rebellious anger in a way that Leo never did, or in fact, could.

104

"That's a good one," he mocked. "Save us from starvation! And what did they do to my own grandmother, that had to sweat and tear on a rack-rented farm for her ten children? To your own mother, and to my mother here, that had a hard cruel life in Limerick when she was young? Who did that?"

He thrust his face down into his father's face. "Who did it? Who but the English landlords? What did they do to Leo Donnel, but throw him into jail three times because he dared to rise against them?"

His father staggered to his feet, pale with rage.

"Leo Donnel is a common criminal and nothing else, and he'll suffer for it. I put him into jail before, and I'll put him into jail again."

The children were shrinking, all pale, to the sides of the kitchen. A dim rattle of rifle fire echoed in a distant street.

"You put him into jail?"

"Denis! Johnny! Denis!"

"So that's what Johno meant by calling me the son of a spy? You put him into jail, and you're proud of it. You spy on your own uncle?"

"Silence, boy!" his father cried.

"And now he's fighting up there in Dublin—"

His father struck him across the face. Then the red smear on his bandage began to spread, and he staggered. The boy held his hand to his face; tears of rage came into his eyes.

"You spy!" he choked. "You spy on your own people."[5]

This moment of revelation and revulsion begins Denis's new life as himself. Ironically, the moment also symbolizes Leo's fulfillment more than does his participation in the Easter Rising. It is not just that he is avenged upon his enemy through his enemy's son, but that his life is finally understood, sympathized with, and found to be of value by a young person of intelligence and potential. Denis is not a hero, but he represents the integration of freedom and awareness that is the beginning of nobility.

When his virtues are added to those of Leo, an image of the fully realized revolutionary personality emerges. It is part of O'Faolain's purpose to show how one generation fulfills another's struggle for liberation. Yet, he also suggests that for Denis the challenge will change, and that liberation will always be an endless process. *A Nest of Simple Folk* ends with young Denis setting out on his own, but having achieved nothing more than that setting out.

O'Faolain often adopts this technique of combining two characters to produce an image of wholeness. In an ironical suggestion of cultural fusion, he marries old aristocratic Henn of Henn Hall, a decrepit Anglo-Irish rake, to robust young Gypsy, a tinker's daughter, in his well-known early story, "Midsummer Night Madness." They make a comical but suitable couple.

> One night two months or so later we heard in our backyard bedroom that a strange pair left Cork for Dublin that afternoon on the Mail Express, all their dozen or so of trunks and bags labeled foward to an address in Paris. The woman, in massive hat with a scarlet feather, had flaunted her way to her carriage — the old man, her husband, hobbling and shuffling along yards behind her.[6]

Here is culture trailing along after fecundity, and ignorant strength taking its first steps toward self-consciousness.

O'Faolain's love stories are often variations on the unity-of-being theme. Of the later examples, two which stand out in this regard are "Foreign Affairs" and "An Inside Outside Complex."[7] Both are stories of ageing bachelors who undergo the rigors of late courtship, overcoming their fears of women, sex, and their habits of evasion. Their women release them to themselves and the world, completing them as cultural beings. These comic-ironic love tales descend from early works — like "Midsummer Night Madness" and "The Samll Lady" — which use love affairs as symbolic links between cultural groups. The later tales emphasize personal rather than intersocial adaptation.

This unity of being motif owes its origins to Yeats, but it becomes highly personalized in O'Faolain's career. Like Yeats, O'Faolain has an intellectually various mind and is pleased by combinations of low and high life, physical and abstract experience. Like Yeats, he shows a fondness for devices that draw antithetical spirits together.

O'Faolain resembles Yeats in intellectual elasticity, in his veneration of individuality, and in his avid search for aesthetic experience. These qualities work against didactic moralism. Though both writers concern themselves with the social order, their moral judgements are as much an aspect of their personal aesthetics as of general ethics. For example, in "Easter, 1916" Yeats vacillates between consideration of the large moral dilemmas of the Rising and personal, emotional response—and finally emphasizes the latter. Personal feeling is given highest priority and is felt to be most inclusive. O'Faolain follows the same kind of pattern in a number of his works. For example, "The Patriot" is a story which also deals with the opposition between politics and personal life. O'Faolain handles the moral consequences of that opposition throughout the story, but ends on personal, emotional grounds.

> Over his shoulder he could see her pale form in the dim light, but where he stood by the window with one hand raised to the blind his eyes fell on the passing car. He saw the white hair of their orator friend, the old bachelor, the patriot, driving out of town into the country and the dark night. The hedges would race past him; the rabbits skip before his headlights on the road; the moths in the cool wind would fly round his flushed face and his trembling hands. But that wind would not for many miles cool the passion in him to which he had given his life.
> "Bernard," she whispered again, and her voice trembled a little.
> He drew the blind down slowly, the lamp shadowing the framework of the window on it, and slowly he turned to her where she smiled to him in the dark.[8]

Each side (the lone revolutionary and the lovers) has its romance. O'Faolain ends his story on a passionate note, placing the moral conflict within the world of personal feeling rather than emphasizing the moral alone.

The early works, *Midsummer Night Madness* and *A Nest of Simple Folk* most particularly, are the obvious places in which to find Yeatsian influence. Yet, it is Yeats's creative temperament more than any stylistic technique or thematic particular that has its most durable effect on O'Faolain. In stylistic and thematic matters, Corkery, Moore, and Joyce were his most influential Irish predecessors.

I have already suggested that some of O'Faolain's works are thematically opposed to particular works by Daniel Corkery, especially those which deal with Irish political conflict. In Corkery's fiction, the Troubles are a period of Irish spiritual regeneration while in O'Faolain's they are a time of personal crises set against the social chaos. Even the titles of their story collections dealing with that period reveal a different thematic emphasis. Corkery's *The Hounds of Banba* (1919) and O'Faolain's *Midsummer Night Madness* are counterparts in the early careers of both writers. Corkery's title commemorates the warrior spirit of ancient Ireland revisited in modern Irish revolutionaries (the hounds). O'Faolain's evokes the rudderless romanticism and essential disorder of the revolutionary period. Speaking for his own generation of Irish writers, O'Faolain comments:

> We loved *The Hounds of Banba*, stories of the Irish revolution, as long as we were elated by being young revolutionaries ourselves, but the more we saw of revolution the less we liked Corkery's lyric, romantic, idea of revolution and revolutionaries.[9]

Romantic nationalism is scrutinized in O'Faolain's work, but it is not wholeheartedly endorsed as it is in Corkery's.

This kind of thematic oppostion masks some stylistic and tonal similarities between the two writers, however. O'Faolain admired Corkery's early fiction, particularly the quiet but lyrical descriptions in the novel *The Threshold of Quiet* and the urban folk realism of "The Cobbler's Den" tales from *A Munster Twilight*. His own early works owe something to Corkery's description and dialogue, particularly in the handling of Cork and environs, and the Cork simple folk.

Corkery's atmospheres of rain, wind, and darkness find their way into *Midsummer Night Madness, A Nest of Simple Folk, Bird Alone*, and other early O'Faolain works, not merely as background to events but as motifs symbolizing the desolation of provincial loneliness. The blinding rains and moonlit precipices of Corkery stories such as "Storm Struck" and "The Stones" are recaptured in O'Faolain's "Fugue," for example. The story develops a hunted rebel's isolation, fear, and loneliness, an emotional complex mindful of some of Corkery's characterizations. The opening description begins this development.

The clouds lifted slowly from the ridge of the mountains and the dawn-rim appeared. As I stooped low to peer over the frame of the little attic-window I whispered to Rory that it was pitch dark; and indeed it was far darker than the night before when we had the full moon in the sky. Rory leaned upon one elbow in bed, and asked me if I could hear anything from beyond the river.

The damp of the dawn was everywhere that I might look. It softened the lime-gable of the outhouse beneath me, it hung over the sodden hay in the barn and, like the fog and mist last night under the blazing moon, it floated over the rumbling river to my right. I could imagine the flow taking strange courses in its flood, swishing, in this neither dawn nor day nor dark, through all the alders and the reeds and the rushes and, doubtless, covering the stepping stones that we hoped would give us an escape to the mountains beyond.

So I whispered to Rory that I could only hear the water falling in the weirs, and tumbling out of his bed he called a curse from Christ on the whore of a river that was holding us here to be plugged by the Tans for a pair of Irish bitches.[10]

In its lush imagery, its extended rhythms, its tropes and alliterations, this passage is a sampling of O'Faolain's early romantic writing at full flood. It seems an attempt to out-Corkery Corkery. Certainly the physical and emotional environment resembles the older writer's, though the passage ends with a dramatic vigor that is more typical of O'Faolain.

O'Faolain's rebel is a more sophisticated characterization than is common in Corkery. His struggles with the environment and himself are seized from within, whereas Corkery tends to objectify the character caught in crisis, seeing him as part of the visual spectacle. Yet, in the brief dialogue exchanges of "Fugue" and several other early O'Faolain pieces, the Corkery influence again reveals itself. Here is one from "Fugue":

Stooping again she replaced the pot and went to sit on the other side of the little boy, and laying one hand on his knee spoke to him.

"That fir Tom brought last night has no fire in it."

" 'Tis a bad fire, God bless it."

"Get a good log, now Jamesy, will you? Will you?"
The little fellow looked at us only, and said, "I will,"
but he did not stir. The old woman broke in irritably:
"Wisha, Jamesy couldn't."
"Indeed, Jamesy is a great man, isn't he, Jamesy?
Imagine Jamesy not to be able to carry a baulk of fir!
Will you, Jamesy?"[11]

These are West Cork peasants, speaking in bursts of folk dialect. The writer's emphasis is on folk realism rather than on a Synge-like improvisation for poetic effect. Full of commonplace matter, idiomatic interruptions, and repetitions, this speech seems to circle in upon itself, implying a particular way of life away from the world's influence. As in Corkery's dialogue, the energy of the vocal outbursts suggests an intense people, while their brief and mundane statements suggest a kind of paralysis. In both writers this conflict between soul and environment is central and it is often implied through dialogue.

O'Faolain describes Corkery's *The Threshold of Quiet* as "delicate, brooding, sensitive, tragic, not without a grotesque note . . . ."[12] These tonal qualities attracted O'Faolain as a young writer. *Bird Alone*, for example, can be considered his revision of *The Threshold of Quiet*. He uses some of the same tools in analyzing the claustrophobic aura of Cork, yet extending the interpretation by questioning the necessity of that claustrophobia. The elegaic descriptions of Cork city, rendered through the vision of Corney Crone, are indeed like Corkery's, and can be felt as "brooding, sensitive, tragic, not without a grotesque note."

An hour before dawn in winter, if the weather is good, an hour after it in summer, I go down along the river where I can see the formless fan of daylight upspreading below the lochs of the Lee, while about me the mist is barely beginning to move from the sluggish mudflats—that dull, whispering, sheeny mirror to the houses across the water, to the limestone castle, to the ball of light risen for another day's toll. There I turn and look up the stinking river at the cold chimneys of the city, where two spires of a triad—broken trident of a cathedral—catch the light.[13]

110

This is Corney Crone's Cork as he sees it in old age. When the young O'Faolain chose to be meditative, he tended to write somewhat like Corkery. He found more firey models in George Moore's emotional and James Joyce's intellectual confrontations with Ireland.

O'Faolain did not think Moore a great artist. He considered his elder so romantically fascinated with his own ego that he was deficient as an observer of life, and so concerned with maintaining a graceful style that he was neglectful of the subtleties of actuality. In general, there was too much posing in Moore to satisfy O'Faolain.[14] Yet, he was interested and affected by Moore's choice of subjects, techniques, and artistic stance.

The primary similarity between Moore and O'Faolain is in their sensitivity to the conflicts between ego and environment. In his *The Untilled Field* (1903) and *The Lake* (1905), Moore protrayed the rural Irish as a morally repressed, culturally thwarted society living in a picturesque but decadent countryside. Into that generally hopeless world he places exceptional or unorthodox individuals who struggle for personal liberation, either through amorous or intellectual pursuit. These motifs have been dominant in Irish fiction since Moore, and they are of decided consequence in O'Faolain's writing. O'Faolain's "A Broken World," for example, with its rebel priest frustrated by an intractable peasantry, could fit into Moore's *The Untilled Field* without violating its method or spirit. Reminders of Moore show up in O'Faolain's later work also. "Of Sanctity and Whiskey," for example, a satiric tale from *The Talking Trees*, is very Moore-like in its ironic depiction of an angry artist confronting arrogant religious authority. These and other O'Faolain stories extend motifs which Moore helped to establish.

Generally, these Moore-echoes in O'Faolain are satiric or lyric, or both. O'Faolain's satires on Church conservatism are reminiscent of Moore's, though they are less blatantly anticlerical. Even O'Faolain's worst priest, the tyrranical Lispeen of "The Man Who Invented Sin," has a human side, while many of Moore's priests do not. It is ultimately revealed that Lispeen has some affection for the young monks and nuns he has bullied, while Moore's Father Maguire, of "Some Parishoners," is a generally evil person, not only tyrannical, but avaricious and vain. O'Faolain is as vigilant against moral compulsion as Moore is, but he sees it as a complex problem,

111

not the satirist's clay pigeon that Moore sometimes makes of it. In fact, O'Faolain's moral bullies often do more damage to themselves than to others.

Moore is less merciful when he satirizes ignorant common folk. O'Faolain depicts their ignorance, satirizes it, yet pities the prisoners of that ignorance, and hopes for a liberation. Moore's "Home Sickness" envisions an almost terrifying intellectual stagnation among the country people; whereas in most O'Faolain treatments of Irish rural life, such as in "A Letter," there is a sense of impotence and incompleteness about the country people, but there is an attractiveness about them also.

In dealing with provincial Ireland, O'Faolain seems to follow Moore in the way he combines social satire with pastoral lyricism. Both writers wish to balance their controversialist tendencies against aesthetic distancing, for both wish to acknowledge the beauty of the Irish countryside. The quiet landscapes of O'Faolain's "Lady Lucifer," or of "There's a Birdie in the Cage,"[15] for example, give an atmosphere of serenity to tales which are nevertheless strong criticisms of Irish provincialism. In this unusual combining of effects these stories are similar to Moore's "So on He Fares," a Shannon story, and *The Lake*, a novel which fictionalizes Moore's native Mayo. The painterly quality in both writers can be associated with their common interest in the works of Turgenev, whose *Hunting Sketches* was the acknowledged model for *The Untilled Field*, and whose novel, *A Nest of Gentle Folk*, provided O'Faolain with a title and a tonality for *A Nest of Simple Folk*.

Many an Irish writer has set about to capture the bleak, lonely beauty of the west of Ireland, and it would be wrong to insist on a direct link in this regard between Moore and O'Faolain. Yet, they are two of the chief literary interpreters of western Ireland's landscape, though neither writer seeks for the immediacy of the primitivists in doing so. While a Corkery or a Seumas O'Kelly tends to look closely at the rugged terrain, emphasizing its grotesque shapes, Moore and O'Faolain generally favor a distant perspective, working in verbal pastel, as in this passage from *A Nest of Simple Folk*:

On that first evening, and it seemed to him as if it were always so, a frozen canopy of cloud hung over the plain. Far away, beyond the Shannon, its shaggy edges drooped down

in a smoke of rain over the land, and there only could one
see any movement in the banked mass, although the wind
whistled in the alders that grew out of the walls along the
muddy road. That thawing cloud would gradually sweep all
across the coloured plain, depositing its vapour in the
already sodden fields and the browned thatch of the cabins,
until after a slow journey of fifty miles its pall blackened into a downpour on the Kerry mountains.[16]

Distances of grey and brown, of cloud, rain, and mud make their
own kind of beauty here, magnified by a vast quietness.

Both Moore and O'Faolain are fascinated by decadence, the
tonality of age and fatigue in places and people, and an unalloyed
aestheticism in art. Moore is more of a decadent himself. For him,
decadence is a form of anti-Victorianism, a release from the trivial
aspect of utilitarian life. His artist-characters, often scornful of the
concerns of the community, reflect his own attitude. Only two years
older than Oscar Wilde, Moore's career took flight in the 1890s, and
he preserved some of that period's colors in his later work. The decadent Nineties came to O'Faolain secondhand, through, for example, a Yeatsian filter. Like Yeats, O'Faolain is too much of a par-
taker and a prescriber in community life to be considered a decadent. His art reaches for meaning and message, though it leans
toward the amoral, asserting a pleasure-principle above all other
functions, and producing effects that one can sometimes
characterize as uselessly beautiful. He creates a number of decadent
characters and sympathetically explores the decaying force of fati-
gued desire through them. Some of his ageing libertines can be considered decadents, people who have tasted pleasure and have
isolated themselves in its memory. The more plebian people around
them consider them "characters," violators of normal life-patterns
who seem to have become harmless in their eccentric age. Old Henn
of "Midsummer Night Madness," Mrs. Pomfret of "There's a Birdie
in the Cage," and Lottie Black of "Billy Billee" are examples. Both
Moore and O'Faolain make use of the attractions of decadence in
challenging prevailing mores.

Along with the brave examples of Yeats and Joyce, Moore's
unabashed defense of the priorities of the artist helped to establish
aesthetic courage among Irish writers. O'Faolain is never arrogant
about his artist's position in society, whereas Moore generally is, but
he is equally forceful in asserting his loyalties to his calling: ". . . all

any artist should ask of his country is his freedom, and all he should promise it in return is his disloyalty."[17] These words, written by O'Faolain in recent times, seem an epigram to the national experience of Irish writers since Moore's time.

"We have explored Irish life with an objectivity never hitherto applied to it, and in this Joyce rather than Yeats is our inspiration."[18] O'Faolian, speaking for contemporary Irish writers, made this comment in 1952, a time which provided perspective for looking back at the Literary Renaissance, at the revolutionary and postrevolutionary experience, and at the new Ireland emerging from the war years. Given the mythological embroideries of the Irish Renaissance, the heroic aspect of Yeats's great poetry, and the revolutionary fervor of their youthful years, the writers of O'Faolain's Irish generation felt that ultimate literary themes should be poetic themes, charged with emotion. Their disillusionment with the actuality of postrevolutionary Ireland was therefore a challenge to their creativity. How could they be both honest and poetic at once? O'Faolain credits Joyce with showing Irish writers the way. His style of "scrupulous meanness," an uncompromising exactness in handling Irish material, was in itself an inspiration, yet through that style they saw that Joyce had also created a symbolically resonant and poetically evocative vision, fulfilling their need for significance in art. Because of Joyce's achievement, O'Faolain could say in 1952 that "disillusionment is also a form of revelation," suggesting a course for Irish writing at the time.[19]

O'Faolain sees Joyce as a writer who successfully used naturalistic techniques to achieve effects that were well beyond the usual objectives of naturalism. Speaking of *Ulysses* as "the greatest Irish novel," O'Faolain suggests that it records

> a young man's search for something inexpressible by the very naturalistic tools it employs, so that in the end all the characters are dilated into symbols, and the climax is a gesture of no meaning and of every meaning, when, in a nightmare, Stephen Dedalus raises his ashplant and smashes a chandelier to bits.[20]

For O'Faolain and many of his Irish contemporaries, social realism seemed a technical necessity, and Joyce was their master in this regard. Yet they did not think of social realism as an artistic end, and for them Joyce is most significant for these kinds of literary moments, when the inexpressible is evoked out of the stuff of actuality.

The principal symbol emerging from that actuality, Joyce's Dublin, impressed them with its accuracy and its suggestiveness. It was more than mere background to his studies of modern individuality; it was a decaying yet remembering city, itself a characterization out of and into which Joyce's people move. His more impressionistic depictions of urban environment were influential in O'Faolain's early work, particularly in *A Purse of Coppers*, which recalls the atmosphere of *Dubliners*, and in *Bird Alone*, in which the evocation of Cork resembles that of Dublin in *Portrait of the Artist as a Young Man*. Perhaps in acknowledgement of this influence, O'Faolain sent a copy of *Bird Alone* to Joyce. The following passage from the novel depicts Cork as it mourns the death of Parnell:

> Along the quays where the shawled women sat and gossiped you would think nothing had happened at all; but as the word went around, we passed one or two groups talking of him. Then, as we rounded up the hill to Sunday's Well, we heard behind us near the chapel the slow, deep doom of the band. We could see the tattered green epaulettes and the dark facings. It was his own band, the Parnell Guards. They passed over the North Gate playing the Dead March from Saul. The great drummer lashed with his sticks on his drum; the side-drums trembled.
>
> Like heavy feet that clank into a tomb, the notes fell on the chill autumn air. There was no link, no movement from one sound to another. They hung in the brain like dead leaves. The dirge locked the mind as the tawny fog locked the embrace of river and sea. We watched them pass across the bridge, the sound growing fainter as they moved slowly out of view.
>
> Mi. Mi. Fa. . . . Mi. Re. Do. Ti. . . . The sounds died along the street, and with a sigh we turned away. A flight of crows lifted up our eyes. Night was still far off. Far behind the empty bridge the unsmoking city had barely begun to twinkle.[21]

Recorded through the consciousness of metaphoric Corney Crone, this impressionistic scene sets a sombre tone for the entire novel, characterizing Cork as a tattered place with a better past, remembering, yet fading into silence and shadow.

Both Joyce and O'Faolain build a fascination out of the slow decay of their cities, setting off moments of individual destiny against the dingy backgrounds of Dublin's brown streets and Cork's foggy lanes. These urban images symbolize the moral environment in which characters like Stephen Dedalus and Corney Crone move, seeming to struggle against a palpable enemy as they seek themselves. They are life-seekers in a world that seems to be dying, and Stephen could also be speaking for Corney when he curses the Ireland he knows as an "old sow that eats her farrow."

Though he did not share what he calls Joyce's "strong distaste of Ireland," O'Faolain certainly understood and sympathized with Joyce's avoidance of the contagions of nationalism and mob-enthusiasm in his times.[22] In *Vive Moi!* O'Faolain speaks of Joyce as a literary hero, an intellectual adventurer who risked all for his art.[23] That art challenges Irish writers to reach for universality and modernity, two objectives of which O'Faolain approves.

O'Faolain's work is part of a generational change in modern Irish literature, yet his part in that change is unique. A way of seeing this relationship is to compare and contrast his creative work with that of three of his contemporaries: Frank O'Connor, with whom he has the most in common; Liam O'Flaherty, a primitivist whom he greatly admires; and Patrick Kavanagh, a poet who deals with many of the same social issues.

O'Faolain and O'Connor have more in common than their very similar backgrounds as poor boys of Cork, their revolutionary experiences throughout the Troubles, their roles as outspoken social critics in postrevolutionary times, their Irish scholarship, and their masterships of the short-story genre.

They are the two most notable figures in a transitional phase in modern Irish literature from a rural, idealistic emphasis to an urban, realistic one. As transitional writers, they retain some of the lyricism that characterizes the Yeatsian era, yet decidedly shift the focus toward their own more prosaic world. In O'Connor's words, they are "strayed revellers" of the Irish Renaissance, yet they must also be seen as pathmakers for Irish literature since their time. O'Connor comments:

116

> When O'Faolain and I began to write it was with some idea of replacing the subjective, idealistic, romantic literature of Yeats, Lady Gregory, and Synge by one modelled on the Russian novelists.[24]

The model was sociological as well as aesthetic. Both wished to work out of a sympathetic understanding for the lower orders in Irish social life, particularly for the urban poor. They saw these, their own folk, as only slightly removed from peasant life, experiencing the difficulties of social evolution. In writers such as Turgenev and Chekhov they found a comprehension for simple folk in an unexaggerated tonality that struck them as true to life as they knew it. They also liked the aesthetic recipe of ironic romanticism in a realist style, which, by allowing the writer to alternate between engagement and detachment, characterized him as both common man and artist.

These same objectives and influences make O'Faolain and O'Connor most alike in their early careers. As the range of their subject matter grows, their differences show more clearly, yet they still retain similar interests. Both write about social displacement; O'Connor's "Uprooted" and O'Faolain's "The Silence of the Valley," for example, deal with modern alienation from the rural Irish folk world. Both writers seem endlessly fascinated with the trials of love-initiation; for example, O'Connor's novel, *The Saint and Mary Kate*, depicting a puritan in love, is something akin to O'Faolain's *Come Back to Erin*, which portrays a revolutionary involved in a love affair. Both writers explore the ironies of religiosity mixed with marriage; two fascinating examples are O'Connor's "The Holy Door" and O'Faolain's "In the Bosom of the Country." Both writers deal with moral rebellion; O'Connor's "The Face of Evil" and O'Faolain's "The Judas Touch"[25] build upon this theme through the experiences of children. Both writers, as critics have noted, write about essential loneliness and isolation. Comparisons in this regard are plentiful, one example being O'Connor's "The Teacher's Mass" and O'Faolain's "The Planets of the Years."

Their treatment of the subject of loneliness also reveals some basic differences between them, differences which begin in temperament and end in alternative, if not opposing, aesthetics. In O'Connor, loneliness is a universal malady that even assails the artist himself. It is an affliction that can only be eased by releasing the af-

117

fections in human contact, or in an art that is very like human contact in its intimacy. In many cases O'Connor shows the introverted intellect to be the chief evildoer among people, sacrificing interpersonal relationship to barren ideas. In O'Connor, people who sacrifice love or friendship or kindness to their own minds are usually judged to be morally guilty; their punishment is often a protracted imprisonment within themselves.

O'Faolain's people are in a sense lonely when they are denied or deny themselves an honest engagement with the fullness of life, not merely through the affections but through the entire personality. Enthrallment to a narrow life is chiefly evil in the way it fragments personality, denying self-realization by denying world-realization. Interpersonal contact can be part of the cure, but total liberation is essentially an internal adventure. In both O'Connor and O'Faolian, intellectual individualism is perilous in that it often leads to alienation; yet, O'Faolain usually suggests that it is best to accept the risk for such an end. He believes that the individual mind is capable of seizing the truth and creating out of it; not to engage in this process can be more terrible than alienation from others, for it can end in self-alienation.

In their books on the short story, O'Connor (*The Lonely Voice*) and O'Faolain (*The Short Story*) each devote a chapter to Chekhov. O'Connor dwells upon the pangs and guilts of Chekhov's submerged, isolated people, and shows a writer expressing his own feelings through these characters. O'Faolain particularly admires the balance Chekhov achieves between sympathy and detachment, allowing him to oversee what O'Faolain calls "the inner battlefield" of character. O'Connor emphasizes sympathy; O'Faolain stresses dignity. Human worth is at the heart of the Chekhov vision they both admire, but they see it working in different ways.

One sign of their temperamental and aesthetic difference is the contrasting kind of satisfaction they evoke in characterization. A brief look at two Cork schoolboy stories, O'Connor's "The Idealist" and O'Faolain's "The Talking Trees," can serve as an example. O'Connor's story defines the progress of young Larry Delaney from dreaming idealist to practical participant in the life of his environment. Larry tries to emulate the code of honor he absorbs from English schoolboy stories, particularly by never telling lies, yet never telling on a fellow, and by bearing up bravely under corporal punishment. This is an especially hard program in his shabby Cork school where the boys constantly lied in the most cavalier fashion, where they always put the blame on another fellow, and where they howled in apparent agony when their teacher, Murderer Moloney, decided to mete out "bashings."Larry's strange behavior not only alienates the other boys, it infuriates Moloney, who prefers being lied to, a sign of respect to his brutal authority. Larry gets very little satisfaction out of his self-imposed martyrdom, and he finally gives in to the system of lying, squealing, and howling. It all seems a reversal of Stephen Dedalus's rebellion at Clongowes, for Larry decides finally that the Irish system is superior, and he is welcomed back into the common fold. Though ironic, this ending is entirely satisfactory within O'Connor's view, for he wishes to delight us with the oddities of Larry's individualistic imagination, yet restore him to a healthy contact with his fellows.

In "The Talking Trees," young and naive Gong Gong accompanies his schoolmates on the Daisy Bolster adventure, wherein, as I have retold, the young temptress shows her naked body to the boys. Gong Gong, like Larry Delaney, is a dreamer, so caught up in his vivid imagination that he stumbles awkwardly along with the gang, always subject to the others' ridicule. His reaction to Daisy's nudity is completely unique. While the other boys goggle in licentious shock, his mind short-circuits into poetry, and he wanders off by himself into what is for him an ultimately romantic night. This ending satisfies O'Faolain, though it too is ironic. He makes us see the full absurdity of romantic idealism in this case, which feels no lechery even when it is intended, yet he also captures and celebrates Gong Gong's kindling literary personality, his separation of himself into a personal truth while the others gravitate into thoughtless stimulation. He is a refiner of his environment, recreating it into something memorable, and in this respect he lives alone. Yet, he too ends in perfect health of soul, for he represents the happily engaged personalty at work in the world.

The pattern of achievement for Larry Delaney and Gong Gong is opposite; they pass each other going in opposite directions, Larry toward reassimilation and Gong Gong toward individualism. Neither completely loses touch with either state of being in the process, but the priorities assert themselves. As comedies about young artist-types, these stories express something of their authors' wishes for themselves. For O'Connor, that wish is for an individualism that does not alienate but rather enlivens his participation in the lives of others. For O'Faolain, it is the personal absorption of experience, free of the bias of the crowd, teaching the mind to use life to the fullest.

As they mature as writers, O'Connor and O'Faolain develop distinctive mythologies based on these temperamental priorities. Both writers create a special kind of intimacy which is the chief attraction of their fiction. In O'Connor, it is an interpersonal intimacy, a sharing of laughter and tears by means of casual tonality and disarming honesty. In O'Faolain, it is an intimacy which uncovers the individual soul, evoking the smile or the frown of self-awareness by means of uninhibited wonder and inquisitiveness. We recognize an O'Connor story by the distinctive speaking voice of the narrator, a voice that invites us into O'Connor's created world as if into his home. We recognize an O'Faolain story by dilating situations, crystalized soul-crises that invite alternating participation and detached analysis.

In *Vive Moi!* O'Faolain remembers his friendship with O'Connor and compares their creative instincts. He considers that friendship the most valuable of his early writing years, when O'Connor

> was the only man in Dublin with whom I could talk about the things that really interested me; that is, any sort of prose fiction, its craft, its aims, its living sources, possibilities and limitations.[26]

He thinks of their imaginations as "complementary in many ways," with O'Connor's gifted by simplicity yet subject to the weaknesses of simplification, and his own helped and hindered by his tendency toward complication. He respects O'Connor's mind as "first-class," marvels at his intuitive flashes, and yet sometimes distrusts his unreasonable side. He prefers the O'Connor that is not too humorous, not too escapist, but close to the crude reality he fought with as an Irishman of their turbulent generation.

O'Faolain is often lavish in his praise of the work of his old friend, Liam O'Flaherty. Although he believes O'Flaherty "has more blemishes and more faults than any living writer of his rank," he asserts that "he surmounts them all" with "the immensity of his natural vigour," and "the undeniable fount of his natural genius."[27] For a writer whose effects are so different from his own, this is an interesting affection. I think the basis of O'Faolain's liking for O'Flaherty is a common romantic streak which translates into a respect for the anarchic depths of human nature in their work.

Speaking of people who have interested him, and implying by that interest his subjects for characterization, O'Faolain makes a statement in *Vive Moi!* which begins as follows:

> I am always attracted by that compulsive quality in men and women that makes them follow a dream. It may be a reticent strength or an eloquent weakness. In either case, it is certain to conceal or reveal a good deal about their inmost natures.[28]

With a few exceptions, one of which I shall discuss, O'Faolain's characters bear little resemblance to O'Flaherty's, who express themselves in violent action. Yet both writers create characters who are defined by O'Faolain's statement, characters who experience subconscious turmoil. In O'Flaherty, their subterranean natures goad them into physical activity. They express themselves in symbolical fashion by fighting with natural forces or other characters. In O'Faolain their personal undercurrents rise up within them at critical moments, impaling them there so that they can see the panoramic vistas of their lives. These moments of recognition do not necessarily make them act in any unusual way, but the course of their mental lives alters, at least temporarily.

Unlike O'Flaherty, O'Faolain is as interested in the evasions of natural urges as the urges themselves. The psychological disguises of his characters are much more subtle and interesting in their own right than in O'Flaherty. The remainder of the above-quoted statement from *Vive Moi!* articulates some of this difference in interest and focus.

> When they hang on to the dream to the end, and it becomes a mask that has become a second face, they are by then so much their own imagination of themselves that it is extremely difficult to see the essential private person behind the dream. But if the dream dies in the dreamer you not only sense, even if you only sense the precious problem in the oyster, but you know that at certain emotional tides the crustacean will open to breathe.[29]

In O'Faolain the dream or compulsion itself can be a disguise. O'Flaherty wishes to plumb the instinctual depths of human nature; O'Faolain wishes to explore the interactions between instinct and imagination.

Of all the characterizations in both writers, the ones that seem most comparable are those of O'Faolain's Leo Foxe-Donnel and O'Flaherty's Skerritt, from the novel of that name, published two years before *A Nest of Simple Folk*. Both characters slowly evolve from crude and brutal men of passion into social leaders and revolutionary heroes. That Skerritt's revolt is against a tyrannical parish priest while Leo's is against the British Empire hardly matters; they are cut from the same compulsive mold, grudging against the social authority until they seem personally insulted by its presence. They are men born to fight and to be swallowed up in a fight. They both end their campaigns in impossible underdog positions and become mythologized in defeat. They stand for unfailing courage in otherwise failing humanity, and they represent their authors' revolutionary sentiments.

Courage matters greatly to both writers, for both wish to challenge the limitations set upon human nature by environmental circumstance. Even two light childhood tales like O'Flaherty's "The New Suit" and O'Faolain's "The Trout" concern themselves with the need to be daring on the road to maturity.

Though he is generally no great lover of peasant literature, O'Faolain is most fond of O'Flaherty's handling of peasant Ireland and natural and animal life. He considers *Famine* a great book, a kind of "Irish 'Exodus' in which there is no Moses to lead out the people of Israel, the starving Irish millions . . . ."[30] Praising its intimacy with peasant life, he calls it

> the perfect proletarian novel, because the balance is held between the development of the individual (which the proletarian writer usually neglects) and the power of inexorable circumstances . . . to mold and limit him, and create a persistent tension about him.[31]

O'Faolain respects the actuality of peasant poverty as O'Flaherty does, yet he also shares O'Flaherty's lyrical response to rural landscape and natural imagery. It is probably this latter quality in these writers that Edward Garnett appreciated most. O'Faolain considers

O'Flaherty's stories of animals one of the real triumphs of his writing, an achievement of beauty through "the pure distillation of natural genius."[32] The difference between them as creators of natural environment is also one of focus. While O'Flaherty effectively magnifies his descriptions, O'Faolain excels in the distant perspective, the panoramic landscapes which stimulate reflection rather than reaction. Though the results are very different, physical description is a measure in both writers of their need for beauty and their underlying optimism.

Another writer of O'Faolain's generation who speaks with authority about life on the land is Patrick Kavanagh. Four years younger than O'Faolain, Kavanagh built his poetic vision out of his impoverished childhood and young manhood on a Monaghan farm, a vision that mingled indignation with affection for his roots. He could not sentimantalize that peasant world as he felt the Literary Renaissance had, for he was deeply troubled by memories of barbaric ignorance and crushing conformity. He was equally troubled in his life as an aspiring artist by a shallow-minded materialism he found in postrevolutionary Dublin, so much so that he devoted a great part of his creativity to writing satires on Irish mores. He became more well-known for these than for his lyric evocations of the land.

Yet, like O'Faolain, Kavanagh struggled to maintain a creative affection for this material in spite of his indignation. Both writers' troubled relationships with their culture became part of their personalities as artists, a self-questioning quality that transformed social criticism into social conscience, and social conscience into self-awareness. Both articulated their society's unacknowledged anxieties by taking them upon themselves, integrating social responsibility and aesthetic honesty in a way that was most influential on younger poets and prose writers.

Kavanagh's fine narrative poem, "The Great Hunger," was published in 1942, dramatizing a countryman's repressions and frustrations at a time when Irish Ireland sentimentalities were a well-established part of the political environment.[33] Kavanagh delineates sexual starvation as part of a fearfully conservative agrarian culture, wherein religious prudery, mother-domination, and economic insecurity combine to destroy the life of Maguire, a common man mired in meaningless but perpetual labor. Terence

Brown has suggested that the poem has a particular sociological significance, detecting a growing disturbance in Irish consciousness toward cultural stagnation and its awful effects on individuals.[34] "The Great Hunger" was an eloquent ally to the efforts of O'Faolain, who as editor of *The Bell* was also trying to shake Irish people out of their moral complacency.

O'Faolain and Kavanagh also shared a concern during that same period for the plight of the artist in a society that seemed obsessed with solidifying its economic security. A new native middle-class was coming into its own, replacing a departed or depressed Anglo-Irish power base. Kavanagh, who had come to Dublin hoping to flourish in a literary environment, was depressed by the indifference of influential people to aesthetic expression and angered by the anti-intellectualism that occasionally rose up to defend that indifference. He became something of a "character" in Dublin, an angry farmer-bard excoriating the Philistines. O'Faolain expressed his very similar feelings in a more controlled, productive manner, fully aware that he was engaged in a fight for artistic survival, but more optimistic than Kavanagh was that he would see it through successfully.

The unheroic quality of life around them also struck them as a depressed subject matter, for they were artists with romantic instincts. Their adjustment to this problem was similar, for they developed a greater internalization in their later work, gradually moving away from broad social commentary.[35]

Self-awareness in both writers takes the form of conscious humility combining with a self-delighting humor. That humor grows out of a lyric acceptance of common life. Kavanagh's late lyrics, represented in self-delighting mood by his Canal Bank poems, catch the same kind of emotional sunlight that gleams in many of O'Faolain's later stories. The very titles of three of the *Foreign Affairs* tales convey their funloving vitality: "Something, Everything, Anything, Nothing," "An Inside Outside Complex," "Falling Rocks, Narrowing Road, Cul-de-sac, Stop." The last lines of the first-named of these stories suggest this gaiety.

> I looked at my watch. In a few hours another green sheen would creep over the straits. Another pallid premorning lightsomeness would expand beyond Aspromonte.
> I walked on smiling at the fun the Vivarinis would have disputing over the name of their newborn child.[36]

Here, as in Kavanagh's late lyrics, landscape is transmuted by a personal expansiveness and a glad realization of earth's recreative power. In Kavanagh, this sensibility takes a religious turn; in O'Faolain, it is more secular and much more urbane. Yet both, fearing to be part of an increasingly critical rather than creative trend in their country's literature, feel that their creative humor is a valuable asset to their art. It is a side of themselves that they trust, and it becomes a durable quality in their work.

O'Faolain praised the affectionate vigor of Kavanagh's early farm lyrics before they were collected into the poet's first book, the 1936 edition of *Ploughman and Other Poems*.[37] They seemed genuine to him at a time when he was criticizing others for their sentimental pastorals. Kavanagh, who became a regular contributor to *The Bell*, had a special regard for O'Faolain's self-questioning humor, which he found lacking in most of his contemporaries, even in O'Connor's laughter.[38] The personalities of Kavanagh and O'Faolain seem miles apart in manner, but to a high degree they share a common seriousness and combativeness about their country and its art's integrity.

In an introduction to Neil Jordan's *Night in Tunisia*, a first book by the talented young Irish writer, O'Faolain praises the freshness of the author's imagery, considering it Irish without being parochial, and also expresses his pleasure with Jordan's intense concern for "the things of the mind and the spirit."[39] Though no self-analysis is intended, these qualities are also his own. The vitality of O'Faolain's style and the intellectual veracity of his vision, particularly regarding Irish mentality, are well-known and appreciated by younger Irish writers, who sometimes resemble him, but more often range outward from a base that he has helped to establish. It is always presumtuous to assert influences, and I do not wish to specify O'Faolain's upon younger writers. It is nevertheless suitable to show how his style and vision can be used as a reader's point of departure into contemporary Irish writing.

From the beginning of his career, he has cultivated a complex view of Ireland and the Irish, providing corrections to popular oversimplifications, misconceptions, sentimentalizations, and vulgarizations of the meaning of Irishness. In service to this vision, he has developed an imagery that is both traditional and antitraditional, wherein the talismans of romantic Ireland merge with the prosaic and even ludicrous images of common, contemporary life. In some ways this imagery seems a summing-up of the poetic ambience of the Literary Renaissance; in other ways it explodes that aura and clears the way for something new. O'Faolain's imagery is alternately beautiful, biting, wistful, and humorous. His ironic, sometimes angry, but ultimately affectionate image of Ireland opens the mind to the fascinations of nationality and culture, while his soul-searching but wordly excavations into the Irish personality make those fascinations seem universal in the lives of individuals. By outflanking inherited boundaries between states of mind, sensibility, and the tonalities with which Irish writers had treated them, O'Faolain has contributed to a modernist tendency in Irish writing.

He images Ireland as attractive but inhibited, worth preserving but needing reform. The effect is often satiric, but emphasizing ironical humor rather than pessimistic sourness. In "Lady Lucifer," for example, Ireland is imaged as an idyllic, rediscovered Eden of quiet canals, flapping herons, and musing conversation, and also as a kind of insane asylum for the hopelessly introverted, a land of dreary rains, empty roads, and suffocating loyalties. These grim effects serve as backdrop to the idyllic foreground in which three friends idle away a beautiful summer day. Their well-being is not devalued, but it is questioned. Another more comical example of O'Faolain's ironical Ireland is in the story, "Unholy Living and Half Dying," wherein the country is imaged as an apartment house. An ignorant but pious landlady occupies the shabby but dominating attic floor, and her presence threatens the comforts of an Irish Everyman living below. He, an ageing bachelor, spends his time playing cards, gambling on the horses, and trying to forget his fear of God.

The opening pages of *Come Back to Erin* render the Ireland of the mid-1930s in burlesque, serving as an overture to the story of a romantic Irishman in the modern world. In that scene, Michael Hannafey, a postal clerk in the city of Cork, is being followed by a government agent, for his younger brother is an I.R.A. outlaw. He tries to elude his spy by ducking into the shadowy pews of St. Augustine's Church, but the agent enters and kneels nearby. A ragged old beggar shuffles over to Hannafey and solicits, in a "curiously refined voice," for the Chinese missions. Hannafey, with his mind on the agent, reacts with sarcastic scepticism but tolerates the beggar's patter. Meanwhile, in the loft, an organ tuner is testing the keys, filling the church with sporadic blasts of outrageous noise. The beggar, unsuccessful, notices a copy of Maupassant in Hannafey's possession, and changes his tonality from pious reverence to lewd suggestiveness. The agent, keeping them under his eye, makes a silent tour of the stations of the cross. Hannafey invites the beggar for a drink, and they sneak out of the church, which is still resounding with the organ noise.

The scene, worthy of a Brendan Behan farce, symbolizes a schizophrenic mixture of Irish politics, religion, and social life. By its intricate but humorous rendering it likens that schizophrenia to an Irish chess game in which everyone knows everyone else's moves beforehand, though despite this knowledge the game goes on resolutely. What O'Faolain is doing is considering old Ireland through a modern, sceptical perspective, showing its absurdities but accepting their staying power.

This is the same attitude that dominates contemporary Irish writing's vision of Ireland, ranging from the tragic visions of Brian Moore and James Plunkett to the comic visions of Benedict Kiely and Hugh Leonard. In the former, the young are often victimized by the failed dreams of their elders; in the latter, those dreams have metamorphosed into a kind of reassuring folklore. O'Faolain is one of the first writers to see those dreams working both ways.

If Irish writers merely complain about their inheritance, they are apt to miss as much as they might if they accept it all uncritically. O'Faolain understands the problems of that inheritance but recognizes the need for balance and modernity. In his "Dyed Irish" essay he comments:

> . . . while I sometimes think sadly that our graveyards may
> be full of mute inglorious Ibsens, Balzacs or Joyces, gagged
> by history, it is more hopeful and profitable to look at our
> younger writers like O'Brien, Higgins, Broderick or
> M'Gahern, and to wonder if we may not see in them the
> beginnings of MacIbsen, casting a cold and vengeful eye not
> so much on our glorious past as on our rather less glorious
> present.[40]

Present troubles may be rooted in history, but the troubles themselves must be faced as much or more than the history behind them. The image of Ireland in O'Faolain's fiction is always remak-

ing itself, taking on new complexities and emanations. In this alone
he challenges contemporary writers to rethink their material.

His intellectual seriousness, his care for "the things of the mind
and spirit," can serve as introduction to the more meditative of the
younger writers. The variousness of his characters, and the
variousness within them, are the chief vehicles of that intellectualism. His people come from all levels of society and many walks of
life, and through their various perspectives O'Faolain tests the
capacity of his own understanding and sympathy. In "The Gamut of
Irish Fiction" he remarks that

> for many Irish writers life exists on a small number of planes
> and their stories are lighted only from a few angles. Chekhov
> has stories of all sorts, but it is not that. Tolstoy can write
> both "Ivan Ilyitch" and *War and Peace*, but it is not that.
> Maupassant can write of peasants and princesses, but it is
> not that—though variety is lovely. It is that the *con-*
> *sciousness* of the existence of many modes of life, and some
> intimacy with them, hightens the treatment of any one
> mode of life . . . .[41]

Perhaps more than any other Irish writer of his generation,
O'Faolain has multiplied the lighting angles, expanding upon an
established subject matter from within and without. His consciousness of a wide variety of life modes is apparent throughout his
work. One small illustration is his story entitled "Lord and Master."

In that tale, the Lord is Carew, the Anglo-Irish owner of
Carewscourt, a grand but fading Big House overlooking the town of
Rathvilly; the Master is Kennedy, a retired school-teacher and
Republican patriot. Master Kennedy thinks of Lord Carew, whom he
does not personally know, as his natural enemy, and, when
Carewscourt Lake overflows into his own property, tries to mobilize
the town officials to act against Carew. The story ultimately reveals
the eccentric idealism and loneliness of both men in a world that has
grown indifferent to their old causes. For Carew, that cause is a
humble dedication to the beauty of Carewscourt. For Kennedy, it is
undaunted courage against oppressors. They are both virtuous men,
and they even tend toward each other's level of life, Carew toward
the dignity of the humble man, Kennedy toward that of the
aristocrat. In physical terms, both are defeated old men, for Carew
will give up Carewscourt and Kennedy will no longer sally forth to

meet the mythical enemy. Yet, they do meet in truce at story's end, and when Kennedy looks upon Carewscourt Lake for the first time, they cross over into each other's feelings and understandings.

> He stopped. Behind the haze of fishing flies on Carew's tweed hat he saw an oblong sheet of water burning below its low granite coping, fiery in the sun that was sinking between a rosy scallop of clouds and the flowing hills of Villy, now as hard as jewels in the cold April air. Its long smooth glow was broken only by a row of cypresses at its far end, the reflection of whose black plumes plunged into the burning pool to spear the light again. Beneath them were two wrestling Tritons from whose mouths two fountains rose, and crossed and fell with a soft splash. Carew watched the old man's eyes for a moment or two. They were a play of astonishment, delight, and hate.[42]

The two wrestling Tritons suggest Carew and Kennedy, showering their idealisms upon their own solitude.

By showing similarities between apparently opposing perspectives, O'Faolain suggests the various potential of any one perspective. Through complex natures he examines the complexity of life itself, realizing that despite the artist's desire for meaning through form there is no "consistent pattern in any man's life."

> Man is not a roll of wallpaper. He is not homogeneous. He is a multitude of particles, full of their contradictions, inconsistencies and incompatibilities that are our effort to adapt to change, to chance, to fate, to unforseen experiences, to new discoveries and to our own manifold mistakes.[43]

And so the patterns must be found in a welter of multiplicity, for, as he says of one of his characters in "I Remember! I Remember!":

> But this was years ago, and since then Mary's life has stopped being the flowing, straightfoward river it once was. Not that life ever is like a river that starts from many tributaries and flows at the end straight to the sea; it is more like the line of life on my palm that starts firmly and frays over the edge in a cataract of little streams of which it is impossible to say where each began.[44]

O'Faolain exploits his characters' confusion about themselves and their lives, their inability to exactly and finally know who they are and what they believe. They engage us in their mental and spiritual searches, or entice us by their evasions.

An example of the former is in "Lovers of the Lake," a portrayal of adulterous lovers who vacillate between belief and scepticism about everything from their accountability to God to their love for each other. Yet, they are courageous self-seekers, and they bare more than their penitential feet on their pilgrimage to Lough Derg. An example of how spiritual confusion leads to a kind of evasion is "The Younger Generation," a tale from *I Remember! I Remember!* which recalls Chekhov's "The Bishop." In O'Faolain's story an old Irish bishop fails to conciliate or guide a modern, well-to-do Irish family, leading him to question his usefulness as a man of the church. He is also depressed by the family's lack of personal regard for him as a man, though he is treated with courteous and formal respect. By the story's end we find that he is more comfortable thinking about his beloved dead mother than of these moderns with all their warring desires.

O'Faolain's theme of difficult belief creating uncertain identity is a durable one in contemporary Irish fiction, where it takes on a darker tonality than in his work. The art of James Plunkett, John McGahern, William Trevor, and Maurice Leitch, for example, roots in crises of the mind and heart leading to self-doubt. Their characters have trouble believing in God, country, love, and themselves, and they tend to drift because of their scepticism (there are some notable exceptions in Trevor). O'Faolain's people tend to alter their beliefs to accomodate their scepticism, and by their struggle to believe despite their disbelief they often construct their personalities on a positive level. Scepticism in such writers as McGahern, Brian Moore, and Edna O'Brien produces melancholy humor, whereas in O'Faolain it is generally hopeful. To him, uncertainty about one's identity is something of a natural condition. It is not a despicable predicament, and it is certainly better than a purely inherited, unalterable status.

If indeed an inheritance is unalterable, it is valueless to O'Faolain. The complexity and change in life call for constant adaptation, most commonly expressed in his work in some form of cultural growth. Contemporary Irish writers favor this same attitude. Jennifer Johnston is an example of one who writes psychological novels about people with powerful historical inheritances; their humanity is measured by their desire and ability to extend outward from their given identities toward those of others. The work of Bernard MacLaverty runs along a similar line, as does that of a number of artists who deal with the sectarian conflict in Northern Ireland.

The yearning for cultural growth, and the mental challenges that come with that growth, are major themes that O'Faolain has helped to establish in Irish literature. These themes were part of the literature before him, but he has intellectualized them more thoroughly than any other modern Irish writer. In his fiction the yearning for cultural growth takes several forms, often imaged in foreign places or in the trappings of high art. These images of the unusual and the exceptional echo back to George Moore and Joyce, multiply in O'Faolain, and filter into the stream of contemporary Irish fiction. For example, the continental tastes of Joyce's Gabriel Conroy ("The Dead") are related to the Parisian longings of Corkman Michael Hannafey, the Maupassant-reading postal clerk of *Come Back to Erin*, and one can extend their connection to a young girl's desire, in Edna O'Brien's *A Pagan Place*, to open a long-saved can of cling peaches in her parents' kitchen. Caught in a limited and conservative cultural environment, the life-seekers search for escape routes. The unusual allures them. This is the essence of O'Faolain's foreign affairs motif, current in his entire fictional career. For example, a fine singing voice images this motif in the early story called "A Born Genius," while an Italian holiday keys the same evocations in the later tale entitled "Liars."[45] O'Faolain also explores the foreignness within the Irish nature whenever possible. He is particularly fascinated by the Anglo-Irish strain in modern Irish characterization. Bodkin of "Murder at Cobbler's Hulk" and Georgie Atkinson of "Foreign Affairs" are examples of atypical Irishmen who challenge preconceived notions of Irishness. Several contemporary Irish writers challenge in the same way; a notable example is Neil Jordan, who creates the artistic, Anglo-Irish Vances in his fascinating novel *The Past*.

O'Faolain's considerable contribution to his country's literature can be suggested quantitatively, simply by listing his many fine works in several genres over a fifty-year period. It seems much more suitable, however, to make a final brief comment regarding the spirit of creativity that exists throughout this entire body of work, for his finest gift to his country's literature is present everywhere in these works, not merely in their totality.

In consideration of that spirit, I refer again to the three travel books, *An Irish Journey*, *A Summer in Italy*, and *An Autumn in Italy*. These works generate in an especially pronounced manner the aesthetic gaiety that is essential in O'Faolain's writing. As traveller, O'Faolain partakes in low and high life with equal enthusiasm, and feasts upon the aesthetic impact of landscapes, cityscapes, individual speech, the dynamics of crowds, historical echoes, architecture, painting, forms, colors, and weather. There is more than descriptive power at work in all this abundance of experience. There is a communication of moments of wonder, when the artist's temperament is excited and his spirit is expanded. In these moments he becomes a model of his major theme, the growth into life of the individual mind and spirit.

In a writer who is so sensible and steady in his judgements, this aesthetic gaiety produces a strong positive effect. In the face of all limitations and pessimisms, he shows us that aesthetic optimism is not only possible but effectively powerful. His art is an act of faith in the embodied truth of aesthetic experience.

For modern Irish literature this aesthetic optimism adapts the enthusiastic spirit of the Literary Renaissance to a vision of new experience, an experience that challenges but need not seem alien to the life-seeker.

Notes

Chapter One Notes

1. *Vive Moi!* (Boston: Little, Brown, 1964), p. 13.

2. *The Heat of the Sun* (Boston: Little, Brown, 1966).

3. *Vive Moi!*, p. 72

4. Ibid., p. 43

5. Ibid., p. 29.

6. Ibid.,

7. Ibid., p. 40.

8. *The Man Who Invented Sin and Other Stories* (New York: Devin-Adair, 1948).

9. Ibid., pp. 148-9.

10. *Midsummer Night Madness and Other Stories* (London: Jonathan Cape, 1932; New York: Viking, 1932).

11. (London: Jonathan Cape, 1933; New York: Viking, 1934).

12. (London: Jonathan Cape, 1936; New York: Viking, 1936).

13. *The Talking Trees and Other Stories* (London: Jonathan Cape, 1971; Boston: Little, Brown, 1973).

14. P. 206.

15. *I Remember! I Remember!* (Boston: Little, Brown, 1961).

16. "What It Feels Like to Be a Writer," *The Boston Irish News* 6, 1 (January, 1981): 4 (reprint of a radio talk).

17. "A Portrait of the Artist as an Old man," *Irish University Review* 6, 1 (Spring, 1976): 11.

18. *Vive Moi!* p. 50.

19. Ibid., p. 21.

20. Sean O'Faolain, *An Irish Journey* (London: Longmans, Green, 1940), p. 88.

21. Ibid., p. 87.

22. *The Talking Trees and Other Stories.*

23. Ibid., p. 85.

24. *Vive Moi!* p. 74.

25. Ibid., p. 78.

26. Ibid., p. 87.

27. (London: Jonathan Cape, 1940; New York: Viking, 1940).

28. *I Remember! I Remember!*

29. *The Man Who Invented Sin and Other Stories.*

30. Ibid. I analyze these two stories and Frank O'Connor's "The Mass Island" in "Irish Elegies: Three Tales of Gougane Barra," *Studies in Short Fiction* 19, 2 (Spring, 1982): 163-7.

31. See Eric Cross, *The Tailor and Ansty* (Cork: Mercier, 1942); also Frank O'Connor, *My Father's Son* (New York: Knopf, 1969).

32. *The Man Who Invented Sin*, p. 3.

33. *Vive Moi!* p. 140.

34. Ibid., p. 110.

35. Lennox Robinson, *Curtain Up* (London: Michael Joseph, 1942), pp. 17-18.

36. *Vive Moi!* p. 114.

37. Ibid., p. 131.

38. Ibid., p. 172.

39. Ibid., p. 175.

40. *Corkery, O'Connnor, and O'Faolain: A Literary Relationship in the Emerging Irish Republic*, dissertation (Austin: University of Texas, 1979), p. 62.

41. *Midsummer Night Madness*, pp. 145-6.

42. Both in *Midsummer Night Madness.*

43. *Vive Moi!* p. 201.

44. P. 162.

45. *The Man Who Invented Sin.*

46. *Foreign Affairs and Other Stories.* (Boston: Little, Brown, 1976).

47. Collected in *Midsummer Night Madness.*

48. Pp. 254-5.

49. *Vive Moi!* p. 259.

50. Ibid., p. 260.

51. (New York: Devin-Adair, 1953), p. 15. Also published as *South to Sicily* (London: Collins, 1953).

52. Ibid., p. 16.

53. (London: Constable, 1979), p. 220.

54. D. H. Lawrence, "New Mexico," *Phoenix: the Posthumous Papers of D. H. Lawrence* (New York: Viking, 1968), p. 220.

55. *Vive Moi!* p. 311.

56. For a comparison of Lawrence and O'Faolain as travel writers on Italy, see Louis Tenebaum, "Two Views of the Modern Italian: D. H. Lawrence and Sean O'Faolain," *Italica* 37 June, 1960): 118-25.

57. Pp. 219-20.

58. *Lyrics and Satires from Tom Moore* (Dublin: Cuala, 1929).

59. (London: Jonathan Cape, 1938).

60. Vol. 2 (Sept., 1928): 7-28.

61. *Vive Moi!* p. 316.

62. Vol. 148 (March 5, 1932): 340.

63. P. viii.

64. *Vive Moi!* p. 340.

65. Ibid., p. 351.

66. Ibid., p. 370.

67. Ibid., p. 357.

68. *Spectator* 151 (Oct. 6, 1933): 455.

69. P. 5.

70. *Midsummer Night Madness.*

71. *The Life Story of Eamon DeValera* (Dublin: Talbot, 1933).

72. *DeValera* (Harmondsworth: Penguin, 1939).

73. (London: Jonathan Cape, 1934).

74. Ibid., p. 56.

75. (London: Jonathan Cape, 1937; New York: Viking, 1938).

76. *Rushlight Heritage* (Philadelphia: Walton, 1969), p. 111.

77. *Spectator* 159 (Dec. 3, 1937): 1014.

78. Published as *She Had to Do Something: A Comedy in Three Acts* (London: Jonathan Cape, 1938).

79. (London: Thomas Nelson, 1938; New York: Viking, 1938).

80. Ibid., p. 7.

81. Ibid.

82. "AE," *London Mercury* 37 (Dec., 1937): 218.

83. "This Is Your Magazine," *Bell*, 1, 1 (Oct., 1940): 6.

84. "Monotonously Rings the Little Bell," *Irish University Review* 6 (Spring, 1976): 61.

85. Grattan Freyer, *Peadar O'Donnell* (Lewisburg: Bucknell University, 1973), p. 107.

86. Julia O'Faolain, "Sean at Eighty," *London Magazine* 20 (June, 1980): 22.

87. *Vive Moi!* p. 370.

88. "A World of Fitzies," *Times Literary Supplement* (April 29, 1977): 502-3.

89. Quoted in James Matthews, *Voices: A Life of Frank O'Connor* (New York: Athaneum, 1983), p. 285.

90. "Signing Off," *Bell* 12, 1 (April, 1946): 1.

91. (West Drayton: Penguin, 1947; New York: Devin-Adair, 1951).

92. (London: Mandrake, 1930).

93. *The Short Story* (Cork: Mercier, 1972), p. 97 (Original publishers: London: Collins, 1948; New York: Devin-Adair, 1951).

94. *The Man Who Invented Sin*, p. 122.

95. Ibid., pp. 122-3.

96. Interview comment, Dun Laoire, March 23, 1981.

97. (London: Eyre and Spottiswoode, 1949; New York: Devin-Adair, 1950).

98. "A Portrait of the Artist as an Old Man," p. 13.

99. Pp. 169-75.

100. *A Summer in Italy*, p. 232.

101. *The Short Story*, p. 28.

102. *The Vanishing Hero* (New York: Grosset & Dunlap, 1956), p. 5. (Other Publications:London: Eyre and Spottiswoode, 1956; Boston: Little, Brown, 1957).

103. (Boston: Little, Brown, 1957), p. 311. Also published as *The Stories of Sean O'Faolain* (London: Hart-Davis, 1958).

104. Ibid.

105. P. 63.

106. P. 65.

107. *Newman's Way, The Odyssey of John Henry Newman* (London: Longman, Green, 1952; New York: Devin-Adair, 1952).

108. "Newman's Way and O'Faolain's Way," *Irish University Review* 6 (Spring, 1976); 87-8.

109. *The Heat of the Sun, Stories and Tales* (London: Hart-Davis, 1966; Boston: Little, Brown, 1966).

110. *I Remember! I Remember!* p. 3.

111. Michele Murray, "O'Faolain Remembers," *Commonweal* 75 (Jan. 19, 1963): 441.

112. P. 374.

113. *The Heat of the Sun*, p. 58.

114. *The Talking Trees.*

115. "Sean O'Faolain," *Atlantic Monthly* 199 (May, 1957): 69.

116. "A Story, and a Comment," *Irish University Review* 1, 1 (Autumn, 1970): 89.

117. *The Talking Trees*, pp. 273-4.

118. Ibid., p. 279.

119. (London: Constable, 1980, 1981, 1982; Boston: Atlantic/ Little, Brown, 1983).

120. *London Magazine* 20 (June, 1980).

Chapter Two Notes

1. *Yale Review* 23 (Spring, 1934): 497.

2. Terrence Brown, "After the Revival: The Problem of Adequacy and Genre," *Genre* 12 (Winter, 1979): 566.

3. Augustine Martin makes this point regarding the Irish public at a later period, in "Literature and Society, 1938-51," in *Ireland in the War Years and After*, edited by Kevin B. Nowlan and T. Desmond Williams (Dublin: Gill & Macmillan, 1969), p. 170.

4. *The Great O'Neill, A Biography of Hugh O'Neill, Earl of Tyrone, 1550-1616..* (London: Longmans, Green, 1942; New York: Duell, Sloan & Pearce, 1942).

5. (London: Collins, 1943).

6. *Times Literary Supplement* (Dec. 3, 1982): 1344.

7. *Bell* 8, 5 (Aug., 1944): 378-9.

8. *The Irish*, p. 124.

9. Ibid.

10. (New York: Knopf, 1961), p. 204.

11. Ibid.

12. "Daniel Corkery," *Dublin Magazine* 10, 2 (April—June, 1936): 49-61.

13. Ibid., p. 57.

14. Ibid.

15. Matthews, *Voices*, p. 78.

16. Vol. II (Oct., 1931): 140-2.

17. P.S. O'Hegarty, quoted in George Brandon Saul, *Daniel Corkery* (Lewisburg: Bucknell University, 1973), p. 50.

18. *Ireland Today* 1, 2 (July, 1936): 69.

19. (New York: Viking, 1940), p. 85.

20. P. 29.

21. *Bell* 17, 2 (May, 1951): 46.

22. *King of the Beggars*, p. 29.

23. *The Short Story*, p. 100.

24. P. 174.

25. "The Irish Famine," *Nation* 196 (March 30, 1963): 270.

26. *A Purse of Coppers*, p. 23.

27. "Silent Ireland," *Bell* 6, 6 (Sept., 1943): 458.

28. Ibid., 460.

29. Collected in *The Man Who Invented Sin*.

30. *Constance Markievicz*, p. 174.

31. Ibid.

32. Ibid., p. 130.

33. Ibid., p. 143.

34. Ibid., p. 132.

35. "Roger Casement," *American Mercury* 37 (Feb., 1936): 162.

36. Ibid., p. 161.

37. P. 39.

38. "Rebel by Vocation," *Bell* 13, 2 (Nov., 1946): 98.

39. *Vive Moi!* p. 21.

40. "The Dangers of Censorship," *Ireland Today* 1, 6 (Nov., 1936): 57.

41. "Portrait of the Artist as an Old Man," p. 13.

42. *Midsummer Night Madness*, p. 137.

43. *The Man Who Invented Sin*, p. 17.

44. *Bird Alone*, pp. 10-11.

45. Ibid., pp. 20-1.

46. Traynor's confession is mentioned by James Matthews in *Voices: A Life of Frank O'Connor*, p. 233.

47. *Foreign Affairs*, p. 161.

48. Ibid., p. 158.

49. Ibid., p. 162.

50. "The Gaelic League," *Bell* 4, 2 (May, 1942): 77.

51. P. 157.

52. *The National Being* (New York: MacMillan, 1930), p. 132.

53. "The Gamut of Irish Fiction," *Saturday Review* 14 (Aug. 1, 1936): 19.

54. *Yale Review* 23 (Spring, 1934): 498.

55. "Gaelic—The Truth," *Bell* 5, 5 (Feb., 1943)' 336-7.

56. "The Gaelic Cult," *Bell* 9, 3 (Dec., 1944): 186.

57. "The Gaelic League," *Bell* 4, 2 (May, 1942): 83.

58. Ibid., p. 81.

59. *Holiday* 33 (April, 1963): 72-80.

60. Ibid., p. 80.

61. Ibid., p. 143.

62. *Appreciations and Depreciations* (Dublin: Talbot, 1917), p. 44.

63. *De Valera*, p. 24.

64. Alan, Denson, ed., *Letters from AE* (London: Abelard-Schuman, 1961), p. 197.

65. Avrahm Yarmolinsky. *Turgenev: The Man, His Art, and His Age* (New York: Collier, 1961), p. 213.

66. *Bell* 2, 1 (Apr., 1941):10-11.

67. "Portrait of the Artist as an Old Man," p. 18.

Chapter Three Notes

1. *Vive Moi!* p. 226.

2. *I Remember! I Remember!* p. 60.

3. "What It Feels Like to Be a Writer," *Boston Irish News* 6, 1 (Jan., 1981): 4.

4. "New Writers," *Bell* 1, 5 (Feb., 1941): 61.

5. *Foreign Affairs*, 1976.

6. Ibid., p. 91.

7. Ibid., pp. 91-92.

8. *The Man Who Invented Sin*, pp. 180-1.

9. P. 72.

9. "A Plea for a New Type of Novel," *Virginia Quarterly Review* 10 (April, 1934): 198-9.

10. "Novelists See Too Much," *Spectator* 154 (March 8, 1935): 386.

11. P. 114.

12. *The Man Who Invented Sin*, p. 67.

13. Ibid., p. 68.

14. *Bell* 4, 1 (April, 1942): 68.

15. P. 62.

16. In Francis Brown, ed. *Opinions and Pespectives* (Boston: Houghton-Mifflin, 1964): 270.

17. *The Man Who Invented Sin*, p. 94.

18. *The Talking Trees*, p. 27.

19. P. 126.

20. *New York Times Book Review* (May 12, 1968): 46.

21. *Modern Irish Fiction* (Dublin: Golden Eagle, 1950): 120-1.

22. *I Remember! I Remember!* p. 58.

23. *Bell* 10, 5 (Aug., 1945): 377.

24. *Midsummer Night Madness*, p. 209.

25. "Discord" is collected in *A Purse of Coppers*.

26. *A Purse of Coppers*.

27. *The Heat of the Sun*, p. 121.

28. Ibid., p. 118.

29. Ibid., pp. 122-3.

30. *An Irish Journey*, p. 92.

31. *The Man Who Invented Sin*.

32. *The Talking Trees*.

33. *The Heat of the Sun*, pp. 67-8.

34. *Vive Moi!* p. 247.

35. "The Proletarian Novel," *London Mercury* 35 (April, 1937): 587.

36. *The Finest Stories of Sean O'Faolain*, p. 279.

37. Ibid., p. 283.

38. Ibid., p. 281.

39. *Foreign Affairs*, p. 192.

40. Ibid., p. 201.

41. (Boston: Little, Brown, 1961): p. 24.

42. *The Heat of the Sun*, p. 5.

43. Ibid., p. 11.

44. Ibid., p. 16.

Chapter Four Notes

1. "The Man from Half-Moon Street," *Massachusetts Review* 6 (Spring-Summer, 1965): 636.

2. *Bell* 3, 5 (Feb., 1942): 328.

3. Ibid.

4. *A Nest of Simple Folk*, p. 378.

5. Ibid., p. 394.

6. *Midsummer Night Madness*, p. 55.

7. *Foreign Affairs*.

8. *Midsummer Night Madness*, p. 237.

9. "Daniel Corkery," 52.

10. *Midsummer Night Madness*, p. 65.

11. Ibid., p. 69.

12. "Daniel Corkery," 50.

13. *Bird Alone*, p. 3.

14. In a 1936 essay entitled "Pater and Moore," *London Mercury* 34: 330-8, O'Faolain prefers Pater's individualism, which he considers the product of a more complex perception of self.

15. *A Purse of Coppers*.

16. P. 3.

17. "A Portrait of the Artist as an Old Man," 17.

18. "Ireland After Yeats," *Books Abroad* 26 (Autumn, 1952): 329.

19. Ibid.

20. "Ah, Wisha! the Irish Novel," *Virginia Quarterly Review* 17 (Spring, 1941): 273.

21. Pp. 127-8.

22. "Looking Back at Writing," *Atlantic* 198 (Dec., 1956): 76.

23. P. 145.

24. "The Future of Irish Literature," *Horizon* 5 (Jan., 1942): 58.

25. *The Finest Stories of Sean O'Faolain.*

26. P. 368.

27. "Don Quixote O'Flaherty," *London Mercury and Bookman* 37 (Dec., 1937): 173.

28. Pp. 284-5.

29. Ibid.

30. "Don Quixote O'Flaherty," p. 174.

31. *"Famine.* By Liam O'Flaherty," *Ireland To-Day* 2, 2 (Feb., 1937): 81.

32. "Don Quixote O'Flaherty," 174.

33. Terence Brown, *Ireland: A Social and Cultural History* (Isle of Man: Fontana, 1981): 187.

34. Ibid.

35. See Terence Brown, "After the Revival: The Problem of Adequacy and Genre," *Genre* 12 (Winter, 1979): 565-89.

36. *Foreign Affairs*, p. 52.

37. "Irish Poetry Since the War," *London Mercury* 31 (April, 1935): 549-50.

38. Patrict Kavanagh, "Diary: Being Some Reflections on the 50th Anniversary of Irish Literature," *Envoy* 1, 3 (Feb., 1950): 87.

39. (New York: George Braziller, 1980).

40. P. 47.

41. P. 19.

42. *The Finest Stories of Sean O'Faolain*, pp. 295-6.

43. "A Portrait of the Artist as an Old Man," 10-11.

44. *I Remember! I Remember!*, p. 11.

45. *A Purse of Coppers* and *The Talking Trees*, respectively.

Bibliography

Books by O'Faolain

Lyrics and Satires from Tom Moore. Edited by Sean O'Faolain. (Dublin: Cuala Press, 1929).

Midsummer Night Madness and Other Stories. (London: Jonathan Cape, 1932; New York: Viking, 1932).

The Life Story of Eamon DeValera. (Dublin: Talbot Press, 1933).

A Nest of Simple Folk. (London: Jonathan Cape, 1933; New York: Viking, 1934).

Constance Markievicz, or the Average Revolutionary. (London: Jonathan Cape, 1934).

There's a Birdie in the Cage. (London: Grayson and Grayson, 1935)—story later included in *A Purse of Coppers.*

Bird Alone. (London: Jonathan Cape, 1936; New York: Viking, 1936).

The Born Genius. (Detroit: Schuman, 1936)—story later included in *A Purse of Coppers.*

A Purse of Coppers. (London: Jonathan Cape, 1937; New York: Viking, 1938).

The Autiobiography of Theobold Wolfe Tone. Edited by Sean O'Faolain. (London: Thomas Nelson, 1937).

She Had to Do Something: A Comedy in Three Acts. (London: Jonathan Cape, 1938).

The Silver Branch. Edited by Sean O'Faolain. (London: Jonathan Cape, 1938).

King of the Beggars, a Life of Daniel O'Connell. (London: Thomas Nelson, 1938; New York: Viking, 1938).

DeValera. (Harmondsworth: Penguin, 1939).

Come Back to Erin. (London: Jonathan Cape, 1940; New York Viking, 1940).

An Irish Journey. (London: Longmans, Green, 1940).

The Great O'Neill, A Biography of Hugh O'Neill, Earl of Tyrone, 1550-1616. (London: Longmans, Green, 1942; New York: Duell, Sloan & Pearce, 1942).

The Story of Ireland. (London: Collins, 1943).

Samuel Lover. *Adventures of Handy Andy.* Edited by Sean O'Faolain. (Dublin: Parkside Press, 1945).

Teresa and Other Stories. (London: Jonathan Cape, 1947).

The Irish. (West Drayton: Penguin, 1947; New York Devin-Adair, 1949).

The Short Story. (London: Collins, 1948; New York: Devin-Adair, 1951).

The Man Who Invented Sin and Other Stories. (New York: Devin-Adair, 1948)—same as *Teresa* collection, but with two stories added: "Up the Bare Stairs" and "The Fur Coat."

A Summer in Italy. (London: Eyre and Spottiswoode, 1949; New York: Devin-Adair, 1950).

Newman's Way, The Odyssey of John Henry Newman. (London: Longmans, Green, 1952; New York: Devin-Adair, 1952).

South to Sicily. (London: Collins, 1953)—published in the United States as *An Autumn in Italy.* (New York: Devin-Adair, 1953).

With the Gaels of Wexford. Edited by Sean O'Faolain. (Enniscorthy, 1955).

The Vanishing Hero. (London: Eyre and Spottiswoode, 1956; Boston: Little, Brown, 1957).

The Finest Stories of Sean O'Faolain. (Boston: Little, Brown, 1957)—published in Great Britain as *The Stories of Sean O'Faolain.* (London: Hart-Davis, 1958).

Short Stories: A Study in Pleasure. Edited by Sean O'Faolain. (London: Hart-Davis, 1958; Boston: Little, Brown, 1961).

I Remember! I Remember! (Boston: Little, Brown, 1961).

Vive Moi! (Boston: Little, Brown, 1964; London: Hart-Davis, 1965).

The Heat of the Sun, Stories and Tales. (Boston: Little, Brown, 1966; London: Hart-Davis, 1966).

The Talking Trees and Other Stories. (London: Jonathan Cape, 1971; Boston: Little, Brown, 1973).

Foreign Affairs and Other Stories. (Boston: Little, Brown, 1976).

Selected Stories of Sean O'Faolain. (Boston: Little, Brown, 1978).

And Again? (London: Constable, 1979).

The Collected Stories of Sean O'Faolain. 3 Vols. (London: Constable, 1980, 1981, 1982); 1 Vol. (Boston: Little, Brown, 1983).

Titles in Story Collections

Midsummer Night Madness
"Midsummer Night Madness"
"Lilliput"
"Fugue"
"The Small Lady"
"The Bombshop"
"The Death of Stevey Long"

"The Patriot"

A Purse of Coppers
"A Broken World"
"The Old Master"
"Sinners"
"Admiring the Scenery"
"Egotists"
"Kitty the Wren"
"My Son Austin"
"A Born Genius"
"Sullivan's Trousers"
"A Meeting"
"Discord"
"The Confessional"
"Mother Matilda's Book"
"There's a Birdie in the Cage"

The Man Who Invented Sin.
"The Man Who Invented Sin"
"Unholy Living and Half Dying"
"The Silence of the Valley"
"Innocence"
"The Trout"
"Shades of the Prison House"
"The End of a Good Man"
"Passion"
"A Letter"
"Vive La France"
"The Woman Who Married Clark Gable"
"Lady Lucifer"
"Up the Bare Stairs"
"The Fur Coat"
"Teresa"

The Finest Stories of Sean O'Faolain
"Midsummer Night Madness"
"Fugue"
"The Patriot"
"A Broken World"
"The Old Master"
"Sinners"
"Admiring the Scenery"
"A Born Genius"
"Discord"

"The Confessional"
"Mother Matilda's Book"
"One True Friend"
"The Man Who Invented Sin"
"Teresa"
"Unholy Living and Half Dying"
"Up the Bare Stairs"
"The Judas Touch"
"The Trout"
"The Fur Coat"
"The End of a Good Man"
"The Silence of the Valley"
"The End of the Record"
"Lord and Master"
"Persecution Mania"
"An Enduring Friendship"
"Childybawn"
"Lovers of the Lake"

I Remember! I Remember!
"I Remember! I Remember!"
"The Sugawn Chair"
"A Shadow, Silent as a Cloud"
"A Touch of Autumn in the Air"
"The Younger Generation"
"Love's Young Dream"
"Two of a Kind"
"Angels and Ministers of Grace"
"One Night in Turin"
"Miracles Don't Happen Twice"
"No Country for Old Men"

The Heat of the Sun
"In the Bosom of the Country"
"Dividends"
"The Heat of the Sun"
"The Human Thing"
"One Man, One Boat, One Girl"
"Charlie's Greek"
"Billy Billee"
"Before the Daystar"
"1000 for Rosebud"
"A Sweet Colleen"
"Passion"

The Talking Trees
"The Planets of the Years"
"A Dead Cert"
"Hymeneal"
"The Talking Trees"
"Liars" (revision of "The Time of Their Lives")
"Feed My Lambs"
" 'Our Fearful Innocence' "
"Brainsy"
"Theives"
"Of Sanctity and Whiskey"
"The Kitchen"

Foreign Affairs
"The Faithless Wife"
"Something, Everything, Anything, Nothing"
"An Inside Outside Complex"
"Murder at Cobbler's Hulk"
"Foreign Affairs"
"Falling Rocks, Narrowing Road, Cul-de-sac, Stop"
"How to Write a Short Story"
"Liberty"

Selected Stories of Sean O'Faolain
"The Silence of the Valley"
"Lovers of the Lake"
"I Remember! I Remember!"
"The Sugawn Chair"
"Two of a Kind"
"Angels and Ministers of Grace"
"In the Bosom of the Country"
"The Heat of the Sun"
"Before the Day Star"
"Passion"
"Dividends"
"The Talking Trees"
"Feed My Lambs"
"Of Sanctity and Whiskey"
"The Faithless Wife"
"An Inside Outside Complex"
"Something, Everything, Anything, Nothing"

The Collected Stories of Sean O'Faolain
This collection contains all of the above-named titles plus the following six
    (Vol. III in Constable eds.):

"Marmalade"
"From Huesca with Love and Kisses"
"The Wings of the Dove—A Modern Sequel"
"The Unlit Lamp"
"One Fair Daughter and No More"
"A Present from Clanmacnois"

Selected Essays, Editorials, and Reviews by O'Faolain

Maurice Harmon's *Sean O'Faolain: A Critical Introduction* contains a detailed list of O'Faolain's minor works published between 1922 and 1966. I repeat most of the same items below, excluding several I have not consulted, adding a few that Harmon does not list, including some published since 1966.

"A Plea for a New Irish Scholarship." *Irish Statesman* 5, 10 (Nov. 14, 1925): 296-7.
"Irish and Anglo-Irish Modes in Literature." *Irish Statesman* 5, 18, (Jan. 9, 1926): 558-9.
"The Gaeltacht Tradition." *Irish Statesman* 6, 7 (April 24, 1926): 175-6.
"The Cruelty and Beauty of Woods." *Virginia Quarterly Review* 4 (April, 1928) 208-25.
"Style and the Limitations of Speech." *Criterion* 8 (Sept., 1928): 67-87.
"Four Irish Generations." *Commonweal* 9, 26 (May 1, 1929): 750-1.
"William Butler Yeats: Selected Poems, Lyrical and Narrative." *Criterion* 9 (April, 1930): 523-8.
"AE: Enchantment, and Other Poems ." *Criterion* 10 (July, 1931): 748-50.
"Synge and Anglo-Irish Literature." *Criterion* 11 (Oct., 1931): 140-2.
"AE: Song and Its Fountain." *Criterion* 11 (July, 1932): 725-7.
"Celts and Irishman." *New Statesman and Nation* 4, 74 (July 23, 1932): 93-4.
"New Directions in Irish Literature." *Bookman* 75 (Sept., 1932): 446-8.
"So This is the Pierian Spring?" *Spectator* 149 (Oct. 15, 1932): 477-8.
"Literary Provincialism." *Commonweal* 17, 8 (Dec. 21, 1932): 214-5.
"The Irish Year." *New Statesman and Nation* 6 (Dec. 9, 1933): 733-4.
"Sean O'Faolain." *Wilson Bulletin* 8, 6 (March, 1934): 380.
"The Emancipation of Irish Writers." *Yale Review* 23 (Spring, 1934: 485-503.
"Plea for New Type of Novel." *Virginia Quarterly Review* 10 (April, 1934): 189-99.
"Novelists See Too Much." *Spectator* 154 (March 8, 1935): 385-6.
"Irish Poetry Since the War." *London Mercury* 31 (April, 1935): 545-52.
"The Poor Scholar." *Commonweal* 22, 5 (May 31, 1935): 127-8.

"The Modern Novel: A Catholic Point of View." *Virginia Quarterly Review* 11 (July, 1935): 339-51.

"The Cost of Living in Ireland Today." *New Statesman and Nation* 10 (Aug 3, 1935): 156-7.

"AE." *London Mercury* 32, 190 (Aug., 1935)' 361-4.

"Irish Letters: To-day and To-morrow." *Fortnightly Review* 138 (Sept., 1935): 369-71.

"It No longer Matters, or the Death of the English Novel." *Criterion* 15 (Oct., 1935): 49-56.

"The Case of Sean O'Casey." *Commonweal* 22, 24 (Oct. 11, 1935): 577-8.

"English as it is Spoken.'" *Commonweal* 22, 26 (Oct. 25, 1935): 633.

"The New Ireland." *Yale Review* 25 (Dec., 1935): 321-9.

"Pigeon-Holing the Modern Novel." *London Mercury* 33 (Dec., 1935): 159-64.

"Almost a Great Novelist." *Commonweal* 23, 2 (Jan. 10, 1936): 293-5.

"Roger Casement." *American Mercury* 37 (Feb., 1936): 160-7.

"Daniel Corkery." *Dublin Magazine* 10, 2 (April—June, 1936: 49-61.

"Introduction to Book Section." *Ireland To-day* 1, 2 (July, 1936): 69-70.

"The Gamut of Irish Fiction." *Saturday Review of Literature* 14 (Aug. 1, 1936): 19-20.

"Pater and Moore." *London Mercury* 34 (Aug., 1936): 330-8.

"The Dangers of Censorship." *Ireland Today* 1, 6 (Nov., 1936): 57-63.

"The New Ireland. A Letter from any Irishman to any Englishman." *Yale Review* 25 (Winter, 1936): 320-9.

"It is Raining Over Here." *Commonweal* 25, 9 (Dec. 25, 1936): 243.

"Famine. By Liam O'Flaherty." *Ireland To-day* 2, 2 (Feb., 1937): 81-2.

"The Proletarian Novel." *London Mercury* 35 (April, 1937): 583-9.

"A Holiday in Ireland." *Spectator* 158 (June 25, 1937): 1206.

"The Priests and the People." *Ireland To-day* 2, 7 (July, 1937): 31-8.

"Don Quixote O'Flaherty." *London Mercury and Bookman* 37 (Dec., 1937): 170-75.

"AE." *London Mercury and Bookman* 37 (Dec., 1937): 217-9.

"Sean O'Faolain Replies to Professor Tierney." *Leader* 76 (Aug., 6, 1938): 521-2.

"The Gaelic Corpse." *Leader* 76 (Aug., 20, 1938): 565-7.

"William Butler Yeats." *Spectator* 162 (Feb., 1939): 183.

"W.B. Yeats." *New Statesman and Nation* 17 (Feb. 11, 1939): 209.

"Sean O'Casey Wallops at the Door." *London Mercury* 39 (March, 1939): 561-2.

"AE and W.B.'" *Virginia Quarterly Review* 15, 1 (Winter, 1939): 41-57.

"How the Irishman Talks." *Commonweal* 31, 7 (Dec. 8, 1939): 158-9.

"This is Your Magazine." *Bell* 1, 1 (Oct., 1940): 1-9.

"For the Future." *Bell* 1, 2 (Nov., 1940): 5.

"Answer to a Criticism." *Bell* 1, 3 (Dec., 1940): 5-6.

"On Conversation." *Bell* 1, 4 (Jan., 1941): 5-6.

"Jack B. Yeats." *Bell* 1, 4 (Jan., 1941):33-36.

"A Challenge." *Bell* 1, 5 (Feb., 1941): 5-6.

"From Bottom to Top." *Bell* 1, 6 (March, 1941): 5-6.

"Ah, Wisha! The Irish Novel." *Virginia Quarterly Review* 17 (Spring, 1941): 265-74.

"1916-1941: Tradition and Creation." *Bell* 2, 1 (April, 1941): 5-12.

"Provincialism." *Bell* 2, 2 (May, 1941): 5-8.

"Standards and Taste." *Bell* 2, 3 (June, 1941): 5-11.

"Ulster." *Bell,* 2, 4 (July, 1941): 4-11.

"Our Nasty Novelists." *Bell* 2, 5 (Aug., 1941): 5-12.

"Attitudes." *Bell* 2, 6 (Sept., 1941): 5-12.

"Beginnings and Blind Alleys." *Bell,* 3, 1 (Oct., 1941): 1-5.

"The Gaelic and the Good." *Bell* 3, 2 (Nov., 1941): 93-102.

"Dare We Suppress that Irish Voice?" *Bell* 3, 3 (Dec. 1941): 169-76.

"Yeats and the Younger Generation." *Horizon* 5 (Jan., 1942): 43-54.

"F.R. Higgins." *Bell* 3, 4 (Jan., 1942): 151-3.

"Fifty Years of Irish Literature." *Bell* 3, 5 (Feb., 1942): 327-34.

"New Writers." *Bell* 3, 5 (Feb., 1942): 370.

"Books in the Country." *Bell* 3, 6 (March, 1942): 407-9.

"To What Possible Future . . .?" *Bell* 4, 1 (April, 1942): 1-9.

"Two Kinds of Novel." *Bell* 4, 1 (April, 1942): 64-70.

"The Gaelic League." *Bell* 4, 2 (May, 1942): 77-86.

The Mart of Ideas." *Bell* 4, 3 (June, 1942): 153-7.

"An Ulster Issue." *Bell* 4, 4 (July, 1942): 229-31.

"New Wine in Old Bottles." *Bell* 4, 6 (Sept., 1942): 381-89.

"Third Year." *Bell* 5, 1 (Oct., 1942): 1-3.

"That Typical Irishman." *Bell* 5, 2 (Nov., 1942): 77-82.

"Twilight in Rome." *Bell* 5, 2 (Nov., 1942): 127-34.

"Why Don't We See It?" *Bell* 5, 3 (Dec., 1942): 161-4.

"The Senate and Censorship." *Bell* 5, 4 (Jan. 1943): 247-52.

"Gaelic — The Truth." *Bell* 5, 5, (Feb., 1943): 335-40.

"Drama in Wexford." *Bell* 5, 5 (Feb., 1943): 390-6.

"Ireland and the Modern World." *Bell* 5, 6 (March, 1943): 423-8.

"Antonio Fogazzaro." *Bell* 5, 6 (March, 1943): 475-81.

"On State Control." *Bell* 6, 1 (April, 1943): 1-6.

"Books and a Live People." *Bell* 6, 2 (May, 1943): 91-8.

"The Strange Case of Sean O'Casey." *Bell* 6, 2 (May, 1943): 112-21.

"The Stuffed Shirts." *Bell* 6, 3 (June, 1943): 182-92.

"Shadow and Substance." *Bell* 6, 4 (July, 1943): 273-9.

"Case of the Young Irish Writer." *Commonweal* 38 (Aug 6, 1943): 392.

"Silent Ireland." *Bell* 6, 6 (Sept., 1943): 457-66.

"Personal Anthologies — 1." *Bell* 6, 6 (Sept., 1943): 496-502.

"The Plain People of Ireland." *Bell* 7, 1 (Oct., 1943): 1-7.

"The State and Its Writers." *Bell* 7, 2 (Nov., 1943): 93-9.

"Past Tense." *Bell* 7, 3 (Dec., 1943) 186-91.

"One World." *Bell* 7, 4 (Jan., 1944): 281-91.

"One World." *Bell* 7, 5 (Feb., 1944): 373-81.

"One World." *Bell* 7, 6 (March, 1944): 465-74.

"The University Question." *Bell* 8, 1 (April, 1944): 1-12.

"One World." *Bell* 8, 2 (May, 1944): 93-102.

"Toryism in Trinity." *Bell* 8, 3 (June, 1944): 185-197.

"One World." *Bell* 8, 4 (July, 1944): 277-86.

"The Pleasures and Pains of Ireland." *Bell* 8, 5 (Aug., 1944): 369-79.

"One World." *Bell* 8, 6 (Sept., 1944): 461-72.

"One World." *Bell* 9, 1 (Oct., 1944): 1-10.

"On Editing a Magazine." *Bell* 9, 2 (Nov., 1944): 93-101.

"The Gaelic Cult." *Bell* 9, 3 (Dec., 1944): 185-96.

"One World." *Bell* 9, 4 (Jan., 1945): 277-87.

"Thoughts of a Juryman." *Bell* 9, 5 (Feb., 1945): 369-79.

"One World." *Bell* 9, 6 (March, 1945): 461-71.

"Eamon DeValera." *Bell* 10, 1 (April, 1945): 1-18.

"The Next Geneva." *Bell* 10, 2 (May, 1945): 97-106.

"Principles and Propaganda." *Bell* 10, 3 (June, 1945): 189-205.

"One World." *Bell* 10, 4 (July 1945): 281-90.

"Romance and Realism." *Bell* 10, 5 (Aug., 1945): 373-82.

"All Things Considered." *Bell* 11, 2 (Nov., 1945): 649-57.

"All Things Considered." *Bell* 11, 3 (Dec., 1945): 761-69.

"All Things Considered." *Bell* 11, 4 (Jan., 1946): 877-86.

"Signing Off." *Bell* 12, 1 (April, 1946): 1-4.

"New Short Stories." *Bell* 12, 1 (April, 1946): 76-80.

"Shaw's Prefaces." *Bell* 12, 5 (Aug. 1946): 425-32.

"Rebel by Vocation." *Bell* 13, 2 (Nov., 1946)' 97-113.

"The Priest in Politics." *Bell* 13, 4 (Jan., 1947): 4-24.

" Getting at Which Public?" *Virginia Quarterly Review* 24, 1 (Jan., 1948): 90-5.

"Daniel O'Connell." *The Month* 2, 5 (Nov., 1948): 340-3.

"Romance and the Devil." *Atlantic* 183, 1 (Jan., 1949): 73-75.

"Secret of the Short Story." *United Nations World* 3 (March, 1949): 37-8.

"The Dilemma of Irish Letters." *The Month* 2, 6 (Dec., 1949): 366-79.

"Religious Art." *Bell* 16, 4 (Jan., 1951): 39-42.

"The Liberal Ethic." *Bell* 16, 5 (Feb., 1951): 5-11.

"Autoantiamericanism." *Bell* 16, 6 (March, 1951): 7-18.

"The Death of Nationalism." *Bell* 17, 2 (May, 1951): 44-53.

"The Dail and the Bishops." *Bell* 17, 3 (June, 1951): 5-13.
"The Bishop of Galway and *The Bell.*" *Bell* 17, 6 (Sept., 1951): 15-17.
"The New Criticism." *Bell* 18, 3 (June, 1952): 133-42.
"Ireland After Yeats." *Books Abroad* 26 (Autumn, 1952): 325-33.
"Love Among the Irish." *Life* 34 (March 16, 1953): 140-7.
"Being an Irish Writer." *Commonweal* 58 (July 10, 1953): 339-41.
"The Irish and the Latins." *Bell* 19, 1 (Dec., 1953): 145-50.
"The Irish: Thoughts on St. Patrick's Day." *New York Times Magazine*
    (March 14, 1954): 9, 46-49.
"For the Child—and for the Wise Man." *New York Times Magazine*
    (March 27, 1955): 9, 67-8, 76.
"St. Patrick's Day: Thoughts About Ireland." *New York Times Magazine*
    (March 11, 1956): 17, 78.
"Looking Back at Writing." *Atlantic* 198 (Dec., 1956): 75-6.
"Are You Writing a Short Story?" *Listener* 59 (Feb. 13, 1958): 282-3.
"Ireland." *Holiday* 23 (June, 1958): 55.
"The Flavor of Boston." *Holiday* 24 (Dec., 1958): 92-101.
"On Writing: An Interview with Sean O'Faolain." (Richard Diers)
    Mademoiselle 56 (March, 1963): 151, 209-15.
"The Irish Famine." *Nation* 196 (March 30, 1963): 269-71.
"Fair Dublin." *Holiday* 33 (April, 1963): 72-80.
"The Meaning of Place." in Francis Brown's *Opinions and Perspectives.*
    Boston: Houghton-Mifflin, 1964: 269-74.
"In Search of Sardinia." *Holiday* 39 (Jan., 1966):52.
"Sean O'Faolain's Dublin." *Critic* 24 (April—May, 1966): 14-25.
"And Svengali Was a Reviewer." *New York Times Book Review* (April 2,
    1967): 2, 20, 22.
"Dyed Irish." *New York Times Book Review* (May 12, 1968): 2, 46-7.
"Great Novels." *New York Times Book Review* (March 15, 1970): VII, 2,
    48.
"A Story, and a Comment." *Irish University Review* 1, 1 (Autumn, 1970):
    86-9.
"A Portrait of the Artist as an Old Man." *Irish University Review* 6, 1
    (Spring, 1976): 10-18.
"A World of Fitzies." *Time Literary Supplement* (April 29, 1977): 502-3.
"A Sense of Ireland." *Times Literary Supplement* (Feb. 15, 1980): 172.
"Introduction." Neil Jordan's *Night in Tunisia.* New York: George
    Braziller. 1980.
"What it Feels Like to Be a Writer." *Boston Irish News* 6, 1 (Jan., 1981):
    1, 4.

Selected Reviews of O'Faolain's Books

Midsummer Night Madness
Strong, L. A. G. *Spectator* 148 (March 5, 1932): 340.
Sunne, Richard. *New Statesman and Nation* 3 (March 5, 1932): 297.

A Nest of Simple Folk
Brickell, Herschel. *North American Review* 237 (March, 1934): 280.
Greene, Graham *Spectator* 151 (Oct. 6, 1933): 455.
Quennell, Peter. *New Statesman and Nation* 6 (Oct. 7, 1933): 417.

Bird Alone
Farrell, James T. *New Republic* 88 (Oct. 14, 1936):285-6.
Troy, William. *Nation* 143 (Sept. 12, 1936): 307.
Verschoyle, Derek. *Spectator* 157 (July 3, 1936): 28.

The Silver Branch
Clarke, Austin. *New Statesman and Nation* 15 (Jan. 29, 1938): 178.

A Purse of Coppers
Bogan, Louise. *Nation* 146 (April 9, 1938): 417.
Greene, Graham. *Spectator* 159 (Dec. 3, 1937): 1014.
Reynolds, Horace. *New York Times Book Review* (March 20, 1938): 6.

King of the Beggars
Bogan, Louise. *Nation* 147 (Nov. 12, 1938): 512-3.
Boyd, Ernest. *Saturday Review* 19 (Dec. 3, 1938): 36.
Godfrey, Eleanor. *Canadian Forum* 18 (Oct., 1938): 216.

An Irish Journey
Boyd, Ernest. *Saturday Review* 22 (Oct. 12, 1940): 32-3.

Come Back to Erin
Bowen, Elizabeth. *Bell* 1, 3 (Dec., 1940)' 87, 89.
Marshall, Margaret. *Nation* 151 (Aug. 31, 1940): 175.
Wyatt, E.V. *Commonweal* 32 (Sept., 13, 1940): 430.

The Great O'Neill
Curtis, Edmund. *Bell* 6, 1 (April, 1943): 66-8.
Reynolds, Horace. *Yale Review* 32 (Winter, 1943): 398-400.

The Man Who Invented Sin (Teresa)
Meagher, E.F. *Commonweal* 49 (Dec. 24, 1948): 282.
Saroyan, William. *Bell* 15, 1 (Oct., 1947): 33-7.
Wolfe, Ann. F. *Saturday Review* 32 (Jan. 22, 1949): 17.

The Irish
Reynolds, Horace. *Yale Review* 39 (Autumn, 1949): 169-71.

A Summer in Italy
Hughes, Serge. *Commonweal* 52 (May 26, 1950): 180.

The Short Story
Greacen, Robert. *Life and Letters* 61 (April, 1949): 6-9.

Newman's Way
Fitzgerald, S.M. *New Republic* 127 (Oct. 27, 1952): 20-1.

An Autumn in Italy (South to Sicily)
Hughes, Serge. *Saturday Review* 36 (Oct. 24, 1953): 71.
Pritchett, V.S. *New Statesman and Nation* 45 (Feb. 28, 1953): 235.
Rago, Henry. *Commonweal* 59 (Oct. 9, 1953): 15-17.

The Vanishing Hero
Barr, Donald. *Saturday Review* 40 (Oct. 5, 1957): 11.
Ward, J.M. *Nation* 185 (Oct. 12, 1957): 246-7.

The Finest Stories of Sean O'Faolain
Finn, James. *Commonweal* 66 (July 26, 1957): 428-9.
Gregory, Horace. *Saturday Review* 40 (Mary 25, 1957): 15-16.
Kelleher, John V. *New York Times Book Review* (May 12, 1957): 5, 22.

I Remember! I Remember!
Barrett, William. *Atlantic* 209 (Feb., 1962): 119-20.
Dempsey, David. *Saturday Review* 45 (Jan. 6, 1962): 66-7.
Murray, Michele. *Commonweal* 75 (Jan. 19, 1962): 441-2.

Vive Moi!
Colum, Padraic. *Commonweal* 81 (Jan. 8, 1965): 489-90.
Dooley, Roger. *Saturday Review* 47 (Sept. 26, 1964): 44.
Harmon, Maurice. *Massachusetts Review* 6 (Spring–Summer, 1965): 636-41.
Pritchett, V.S. *New Statesman* 70 (Aug. 13, 1965): 219-20.

The Heat of the Sun
Burgess, Anthony. *Spectator* 218 (Feb. 3, 1967): 140-1.
Dempsey, David. *Saturday Review* 49 (Oct. 15, 1966): 40-1.
Kelleher, John V. *New York Times Book Review* (Oct. 16, 1966): 64-6.

The Talking Trees
Hughes, John. *Saturday Review* 54 (Feb. 6, 1971): 30-1.

Foreign Affairs
Bonaccorso, Richard. *Eire-Ireland* 13, 2 (Summer, 1978): 135-6.
Glendinning, Victoria. *Times Literary Supplement* (April 16, 1976): 455.
Moynahan, Julian. *New York Times Book Review* (Jan. 25, 1976): 6.

Selected Stories of Sean O'Faolain
Davenport, Gary. *Hudson Review* 32 (Spring, 1979): 143-4.
Paulin, Tom. *Encounter* 50 (June, 1978): 64-6.
Tuohy, Frank. *Times Literary Supplement* (Feb. 24, 1978): 236.

And Again
Lewis, Peter. *Times Literary Supplement* (Feb. 15, 1980): 170.
Mutran, Munira H. *Irish University Review* 10, 1 (Spring, 1980): 177-9.
Naughton, John. *Listener* 102 (Oct. 18, 1979) 534-5.

The Collected Stories of Sean O'Faolian
Craig, Patricia. *Times Literary Supplement* (Nov. 7, 1980): 1250; (Nov. 20, 1981): 1350; (Dec. 3, 1982): 1344.
Donoghue, Denis. *New York Times Book Review* (Oct. 30, 1983): 11, 27.

Critical and Related Studies

AE (George Russell). *The National Being*. New York: Macmillan, 1930.
Allen, Walter. *The Short Story in English*. New York: Oxford University, 1981.
Averill, Deborah M. *The Irish Short Story from George Moore to Frank O'Connor*. Washington: University Press of America, 1982.
Bates, H.E. *The Modern Short Story*. New York: Thomas Nelson, 1941.
Beckett, J.C. *The Making of Modern Ireland*. New York: Knopf, 1966.
———. *The Anglo-Irish Tradition*. Ithaca: Cornell University, 1976.
Bloom, Harold. *Yeats*. New York: Oxford University, 1970.
Bonaccorso, Richard. "Sean O'Faolain's Foreign Affair." *Eire-Ireland* 16, 2 (Summer, 1981): 134-44.
———. "Irish Elegies: Three Tales of Gougane Barra." *Studies in Short Fiction* 19, 2 (Spring, 1982): 163-7.
Bowen, Elizabeth. *Collected Impressions*. New York: Knopf, 1950.
Boyd, Ernest A. *Appreciations and Depreciations*. Dublin: Talbot, 1917.
———. *Ireland's Literary Renaissance*. New York: Knopf, 1922.
———. "Joyce and the New Irish Writers." *Current History* 39 (1934): 699-704.
Boylan, Henry. *A Dictionary of Irish Biography*. New York: Barnes and Noble, 1979.
Braybrooke, Neville. "Sean O'Faolain." *Dublin Magazine* 31, 2 (April–June, 1955): 22-7.
Brown, Terence. "After the Revival: The Problem of Adequacy and Genre." *Genre* 12 (Winter, 1979): 565-89.
———. *Ireland: A Social and Cultural History, 1922-79*. Isle of Man: Fontana, 1981.

Butler, Hubert. "*The Bell:* An Anglo-Irish View." *Irish University Review* 6 (Spring, 1976): 66-72.

Carpenter, A., and Fallon, P., eds. *The Writers: A Sense of Ireland.* New York: Braziller, 1980.

Conolly, Cyril. "Comment." *Horizon* 5, 25 (Jan., 1942): 3-11.

Connolly, Peter, ed. *Literature and the Changing Ireland.* Gerards Cross: Colin Smythe, 1982.

Corkery, Daniel. *The Hidden Ireland.* Dublin: Gill and Son, 1956 (1924).

————. *Synge and Anglo-Irish Literature.* Cork: Cork University, 1931.

Cowley, Malcolm. "Yeats and O'Faolain." *New Republic* 126 (Feb. 15, 1939): 49-50.

Cronin, Sean. "Nation Building and the Irish Language Revival Movement." *Eire-Ireland* 13, 1 (Spring, 1978): 7-14.

Cross, Eric. *The Tailor and Ansty.* Cork: Mercier, 1970.

Curtis, Edmund. *A History of Ireland.* London: Methuen, 1936.

Davenport, Gary. "Sean O'Faolain's Troubles: Revolution and Provincialism in Modern Ireland." *South Atlantic Quarterly* 75 (Summer, 1976): 312-22.

Davis, Robert Bernard. *George William Russell ("AE").* Boston: Twayne, 1977.

Denson, Alan, ed. *Letters from AE.* London: Abelard-Schuman, 1961.

Dillon, Eilis. "Sean O'Faolain and the Young Writer."*Irish University Review* 6 (Spring, 1976): 37-44.

Doyle, Paul A. "Sean O'Faolain as a Novelist." *South Atlantic Quarterly* 66, (Autumn, 1967): 566-73.

————. *Sean O'Faolain.* New York: Twayne, 1968.

Duffy, Joseph. "A Broken World: The Finest Short Stories of Sean O'Faolain." *Irish University Review* 6 (Spring, 1976): 30-36.

Ellmann, Richard. *Yeats: The Man and the Masks.* New York: Macmillan, 1948.

————. *James Joyce.* New York: Viking, 1959.

————. *Ulysses on the Liffey.* New York: Oxford University, 1972.

————, ed. *Selected Letters of James Joyce.* New York: Viking, 1976.

Fallis, Richard. *The Irish Renaissance.* Syracuse: Syracuse University, 1977.

Flanagan, Thomas. "Irish are a People Trapped in History." *The Hartford Courant* (May 10, 1981): A1-A28.

Foley, Dermot. "Monotonously Rings the Little Bell." *Irish University Review* 6 (Spring, 1976): 54-62.

Freyer, Grattan. *Peadar O'Donnell.* Lewisburg: Bucknell University, 1973.

————. "Change Naturally: The Fiction of O'Flaherty, O'Faolain, McGahern." *Eire-Ireland* 18, 1 (Spring, 1983): 138-44.

Friedland, Louis S., ed. *Letters on the Short Story, the Drama and Other Literary Topics by Anton Chekhov.* New York: Benjamin Blom, 1964.

Garfitt, Roger. "Constants in Contemporary Irish Fiction." In *Two Decades of Irish Writing.* Douglas Dunn, ed. Chester Springs: Dufour, 1975.

Gibbings, Robert. *Lovely is the Lee.* New York: Dutton, 1945.

Gibbon, Monk, ed. *The Living Torch.* London: Macmillan, 1937.

Glendinning, Victoria. *Elizabeth Bowen.* New York: Knopf, 1978.

Greacen, Robert. "Contemporary Irish Writing." *Life and Letters* 61 (April, 1949): 6-9.

Hanley, Katherine. "The Short Stories of Sean O'Faolain: Theory and Practice." *Eire-Ireland* 6, 3 (Fall, 1971): 3-11.

Harmon, Maurice. *Sean O'Faolain: A Critical Introduction.* Notre Dame: University of Notre Dame, 1966.

———. "Sean O'Faolain: 'I Have Nobody to Vote For'." *Studies* 56, 221 (Spring, 1967): 51-9.

———. "Biographical Note." *Irish University Review* 6 (Spring, 1976): 7-9.

Harrod, L.V. "The Ruined Temples of Sean O'Faolain." *Eire-Ireland* 9, 1 (Spring, 1974): 115-19.

Hickey, D.J. and Doherty, J.E. *A Dictionary of Irish History Since 1800.* Totowa: Barnes and Noble, 1981.

Hogan, Robert, ed. *Dictionary of Irish Literature* Westport: Greenwood, 1979.

Hopkins, Robert H. "The Pastoral Mode of Sean O'Faolain's 'The Silence of the Valley'." *Studies in Short Fiction* 1, 2 (Winter, 1964): 93-8.

Hughes, Douglas, ed. *The Man of Wax: Critical Essays on George Moore.* New York: New York University, 1971.

Jenkins, Hilary. "Newman's Way and O'Faolain's Way." *Irish University Review* 6 (Spring, 1976):' 87-94.

Jones, James Land. *Adam's Dream: Mythic Consciousness in Keats and Yeats.* Athens: University of Georgia, 1975.

Journal of Irish Literature 4, 1 (Jan., 1975): "A Frank O'Connor Number."

Kain, Richard M. *Dublin in the Age of William Butler Yeats and James Joyce.* Devon: David and Charles, 1962.

Kavanagh, Patrick. "Diary. Being Some Reflections on the 50th Anniversary of Irish Literature." *Envoy*, 1, 1 (Dec., 1949): 86-90.

———. *Collected Pruse.* London: Macgibbon and Kee, 1967.

Kelleher, John V. "Irish Literature Today." *Atlantic Monthly* 175, 3 (March, 1945): 70-5.

———. "Sean O'Faolain." *Atlantic Monthly* 199 (May, 1957): 67-9.

159

Kiely, Benedict. *Modern Irish Fiction—A Critique*. Dublin: Golden Eagle, 1950.

Lawrence, D. H. *D. H. Lawrence and Italy*. New York: Viking, 1972.

———. *Phoenix: The Posthumous Papers*. New York: Viking, 1972.

LeMoigne, Guy. "Sean O'Faolain's Short Stories and Tales." In *The Irish Short Story*. Patrick Rafroidi and Terence Brown, eds. Atlantic Highlands: Humanities Press, 1979.

Levander, Marianne. "Sean O'Faolain, Nationalism, and the Gaelic Language." *Moderna Sprak* 72, 3 (1978): 257-60.

Lynch, Patrick. "O'Faolain's Way." *Bell* 18, 10 (March, 1953): 628-31.

Lyons, F. S. L. *Ireland Since the Famine* New York: Scribner's, 1971.

———. "Sean O'Faolain as Biographer." *Irish University Review* 6 (Spring, 1976): 95-109.

———. *Culture and Anarchy in Ireland: 1890-1939*. Oxford: Oxford University, 1979.

McCartney, Donal. "Sean O'Faolain: A Nationalist Right Enough." *Irish University Review* 6 (Spring, 1976): 73-86.

Macauley, Robie. "Sean O'Faolain, Ireland's Youngest Writer." *Irish University Review* 6 (Spring, 1976): 110-117.

McHugh, Roger, and Harmon, Maurice. *A Short History of Anglo-Irish Literature*. Dublin: Wolfhound, 1982.

McMahon, Sean. "O My Youth, O My Country." *Eire-Ireland* 6, 3 (Fall, 1971): 144-55.

MacManus, Francis. *The Years of the Great Test, 1926-1939*. Cork: Mercier, 1967.

Malloy, Ione. *Corkery, O'Connor, and O'Faolain: A Literary Relationship in the Emerging Irish Republic*. Doctoral Dissertation. Austin: University of Texas, 1979.

Matthews, James. *Voices: A Life of Frank O'Connor*. New York: Athaneum, 1983.

Mercier, Vivian. "The Professionalism of Sean O'Faolain." *Irish University Review* 6 (Spring, 1976): 45-53.

Mirsky, D.S. *A History of Russian Literature from Its Beginnings to 1900*. F.J. Whitfield, ed. New York: Knopf, 1958.

Moore, George. *Hail and Farewell!* 3 Vols. London: Heinemann, 1911-14.

Moynahan, Julian. "God Smiles, the Priest Beams, and the Novelist Groans." *Irish University Review* 6 (Spring, 1976): 19-29.

Nobokov, Vladimir. "On Chekhov." *Atlantic* 248 (Aug., 1981): 19-23.

Nowlan, Kevin B., and Williams, T. Desmond, eds. *Ireland in the War Years and After*. Dublin: Gill and Macmillan, 1969.

O'Brien, Conor Cruise. (Donat O'Donnell) "The Unfallen." *Envoy* 1, 1 (Dec., 1949)' 44-50.

————. *Maria Cross*. Fresno: Academy Guild, 1963.

O'Brien, Edna. *Mother Ireland*. New York: Harcourt Brace Jovanovich, 1976.

O'Brien, James H. *Liam O'Flaherty*. Lewisburg: Bucknell University, 1973.

O'Connell, Maurice R. "Daniel O'Connell and Irish-Americans." *Eire-Ireland* 16, 2 (Summer, 1981): 7-15.

O'Connor, Frank. "Two Friends: Yeats and AE." *Yale Review* 29 (Sept., 1939): 60-88.

————. "The Future of Irish Literature." *Horizon* 5 (Jan., 1942): 55-63.

————. *Leinster, Munster, and Connaught*. London: Robert Hale, 1950.

————. *An Only Child*. New York: Knopf, 1961.

————. *A Short History of Irish Literature*. New York: G.P. Putnam's, 1967.

————. *My Father's Son*. New York: Knopf, 1969.

O'Donnell, Peadar. "*The Irish Press* and O'Faolain." *Bell* 18, 11 (Summer, 1953): 5-7.

O'Faolain, Julia. "Sean at Eighty." *London Magazine* 20 (June, 1980): 18-28.

O'Farrell, Patrick. *Ireland's English Question*. New York: Schocken, 1971.

O'Flaherty, Liam. *A Tourist's Guide to Ireland*. London: Mandrake, 1930.

Pritchett, V.S. *Dublin: A Portrait*. New York: Harper and Row, 1967.

————. *The Myth Makers*. New York: Random House, 1979.

Profitt, Edward, "Glimmerings: Sean O'Faolain's 'The Trout'." *Studies in Short Fiction* 17 (Winter, 1980): iii-iv.

Rafroidi, Patrick, and Harmon, Maurice, eds. *The Irish Novel in Our Time*. Lille: University de Lille, 1975.

Rafroidi, Patrick, and Brown, Terence, eds. *The Irish Short Story*. Atlantic Highlands: Humanities, 1979.

Rippier, Joseph Storey. *The Short Stories of Sean O'Faolain*. Gerrards Cross: Colin Smythe, 1976.

Robinson, Lennox. *Curtain Up*. London: Michael Joseph, 1942.

Saul, Goerge Brandon. *Rushlight Heritage*. Philadelphia: Walton, 1969.

————. *Daniel Corkery*. Lewisburg: Bucknell University, 1973.

Shaw, George Bernard. *The Matter With Ireland*. New York: Hill & Wang, 1962.

Sheehy, Maurice, Ed. *Michael/Frank*. New York: Knopf, 1969.

Summerfield, Henry. *That Myriad-Minded man*. Totawa: Rowman and Littlefield, 1977.

Tenenbaum, Louis. "Two Views of the Modern Italian: D.H. Lawrence and Sean O'Faolain." *Italica* 37 (June, 1960): 118-25.

Valency, Maurice. *Jean Giraudoux: Four Plays*. New York: Hill & Wang, 1958.

Warner, Alan. *A Guide to Anglo-Irish Literature*. Dublin: Gill and Macmillan, 1981.

Wohlgelernter, Maurice. *Frank O'Connor: An Introduction*. New York: Columbia University, 1977.

Yeats, William Butler. *Essays and Introductions*. New York: Macmillan, 1961.

———. *The Autobiography of William Butler Yeats*. New York: Collier, 1965.

Yarmolinsky, Avrahm. *Turgenev: The Man, His Art, and His Age*. New York: Collier, 1961.

Index

fall," 49; "Ploughing of Leaca-na-
Naomh, The," 49; "Ruining of Dro-
macurrig, The," 50; "Stones, The,"
49, 108; "Storm Struck," 108; *Synge
and Anglo-Irish Literature*, 20, 50,
51; *Threshold of Quiet, The*, 108,
110; "Wager, The," 49
Craig, Patricia, 46
Criterion, The, 50
Cronin, Denis (Dinny Gougane), 9
Cross, Eric, 56. Works: *Tailor and
Ansty, The*, 56, 134n31
Curragh, The, 8

Davis, Thomas, 47
"Dead Cert, A," 37
"Death of Nationalism, The," 53
DeValera, Eamon, 14, 23, 25, 26,
43, 45, 71, 101
DeValera, 25
Dialect, Irish country, 95, 109, 110
Dickens, Charles, 78
"Discord," 89
Distancing technique, 76-77, 82, 88,
112-113, 123
"Dividends," 37, 46, 92, 93-94
Dublin (city), 70, 85-86, 89, 115,
116, 123, 124; literary period in, 21
Dublin Magazine, 49, 51
Dun laoire, Dublin, 40
Dunsany, Lord, 21
"Dyed Irish," 88, 127

Edward VIII, King (of England), 16
Elegaic mood, 15, 96, 110
"Emancipation of Irish Writers, The,"
43, 69
"End of the Record, The," 95-96
Ennis, Co. Clare, 14

"Fair Dublin," 70
"Falling Rocks, Narrowing Road, Cul-
de-sac, Stop," 14, 66-67, 97, 124
Family life (as subject), 5, 35
Farrell, Michael, 27
Faulkner, William, 34
"Feed My Lambs," 37, 66, 74
Fenian Brotherhood, 63-64
"Fifty Years of Irish Literature,"
102, 103

*Finest Stories of Sean O'Faolain,
The*, 33
Foley, Dermot, 27
Foreign Affairs, 13, 38, 97, 124
"Foreign Affairs," 106, 131
"Fugue," 13, 17, 19, 108-110
"Fur Coat, The," 58
Fusion view of Irish culture, 51, 68,
70, 71, 106

"Gaelic Cult, The," 69
Gaelic League, The, 9, 43, 44, 67,
69-70
"Gaelic—The Truth," 28
"Gamut of Irish Fiction, The," 128
Garnett, Edward, 19-20, 122
Gogarty, Oliver St. John, 21
Gogol, Nicolai, 12. Works: *Dead
Souls*, 12
Gougane Barra (West Cork), 8-9,
13, 66
Greene, Graham, 22, 25, 34-35
Gregory, Isabella Augusta, 41, 42,
117

Harkness Commonwealth Fellowship,
15-16
Harmon, Maurice, 101
Harvard University, 15, 17, 19
Hawthorne, Nathaniel, 49
Hayes, Richard, 97
Heat of the Sun, The, 35, 36,
37, 46, 90, 98
Hemingway, Ernest, 34
Herzen, Alexander, 71
Higgins, Aidan, 127
"How to Write a Short Story," 97-98
Hyde, Douglas, 44
"Hymeneal," 85-87

I Remember! I Remember!, 35, 36,
46, 130
"I Remember! I Remember!," 35-36,
129
Ibsen, Henrik, 127
"In the Bosom of the Country,"
98-100, 117
Inherited identity, struggle against,
24, 42, 83, 92, 103, 104-105,
111, 122, 130-131
"Inside Outside Complex, An,"
Preface, 106, 124